"*You're Doing **What***? is an inspirational and insightful call to action to its readers. These stories are certain to encourage women – and men – of all ages to view aging as an opportunity to act on long deferred or never before-imagined dreams."

– Congresswoman **Barbara Lee**

"How refreshing it is to sample a collection of essays by women of a certain age who ignored biases and barriers that discriminate against women, gave themselves permission to climb steep mountains, tore up the rulebook of tradition, and launched their own search for adventure, discovery, and meaning. Their stories are as unique as each of these women."

– **Eleanor Coppola**, filmmaker, writer, artist

"Marjorie Lasky's book is a revelation, an entertaining read and perfect retort to all who wrongly assume that age renders women useless and incapable. These thoughtful, frank, and inspiring essays by older women show how human spirit can transcend age as they take on new challenges and adventures head-on and full of heart."
– **Helen Zia**, former Executive Editor of *Ms. magazine* and author of the forthcoming book *Last Boat out of Shanghai*

"Being a man who believes women, on average, have more skills than men in the areas that count the most for growing older – intimacy, deep friendship, networking, caring for – I look to women to help define our way forward, just as I have done since the sixties in pursuit of gender equity in family life as well as in the workplace. The kids are grown, work is a memory, where to from here? This book provides poignant stories containing the kind of deep wisdom we need to live out our elder journey, together."

– **Terry A. Kupers**, M.D., psychiatrist and author of *Revisioning Men's Lives* and *Solitary: The Inside Story of Supermax Isolation and How We Can Abolish It*

"To have a 'shout out' for the women over a 'certain age' and how these women reflect their energies, their 'smarts' and their most valuable experiences, is like pushing the 'positive button' for US ALL! Being able to jump up and down with our creative energies and being able to express ourselves is a gift, hopefully to those that follow us!"
— **Inez Storer**, painter and mixed-media artist

"*You're Doing* **What?** busts the prevalent myth that growing older means slowing down and retiring to a rocking chair on some musty porch. These women show that re-inventing oneself is a continual option, even well into those 'twilight years.' Pick this book up to motivate you, at any age, to live life to the fullest."
— **Dale Griffiths Stamos**, playwright, screenwriter, teacher and co-author of *RenWomen: What Modern Renaissance Women Have to Teach Us About Living Rich, Fulfilling Lives*

"Many women of 'a certain age' tell me that, no longer young, they feel invisible in our culture. So, here in *You're Doing* **What?** Marjorie Lasky has assembled sixty-plus women who command their visibility. Lasky writes that these are 'stories by older women' – older than what, I have to ask? Younger than springtime!"
— **Alan Myerson**, film/TV director, teacher, poet

"I plan to use this book as my bible."
— **Stephanie Lee**, investment advisor, jazz bassist, and rock violinist

YOU'RE DOING *WHAT*?

YOU'RE DOING *WHAT*?

Older Women's Tales
of Achievement and Adventure

Collected and Edited by

MARJORIE PENN LASKY

REGENT PRESS
Berkeley, California

[paperback]
ISBN 13: 978-1-58790-454-7
ISBN 10: 1-58790-454-3

[e-book]
ISBN 13: 978-1-58790-455-4
ISBN 10: 1-58790-455-1

Library of Congress Control Number: 2018955184

Cover Design: Naomi Brauner

For further information
www.olderwomenstales.com
www.margelasky.com

Manufactured in the U.S.A.
REGENT PRESS
Berkeley, California
www.regentpress.net

CONTENTS

OVERCOMING ADVERSITY

I NEVER THOUGHT I'D DO THIS

UNPACKING MY BAGS IN ANOTHER LOCALE

Photos: *Authors furnished and gave permission for use of all unattributed photos.*

In text, italicized editor's précis follows each author's title.

Preface

TALES OF ACHIEVEMENT
AND ADVENTURE

Older now, you find holiness in anything that continues.[1]
— NAOMI SHIHAB NYE,
"The Man Who Makes Brooms"

You're Doing What? In my mid-70s, I asked myself what was I doing scrambling off-trail in Sedona, Arizona, traversing slick steep slopes, climbing to intimidating heights, and choosing between the narrow ledge and the prickly pear. Yet each day when the scrambling ended and I was (essentially) intact, I was amazed at what I had accomplished.

Eventually I called it "My Trip of Unintended Consequences" because it inspired new challenges. One endeavor birthed this project – my collecting stories by older women, describing their achievements and adventures. Another led to my own story, "The Inevitable Intrudes," included here.

Tales of creative, daring older women have existed for generations. An Athabascan legend, passed on from mothers to daughters and eventually recorded by Velma Wallis in *Two Old Women* (1994), tells of two elderly women abandoned by their migrating tribe. Overcoming the terrors of starvation and death, the women survived by depending upon their learned but previously unused skills in hunting, fishing, and shelter-building.

Like the Athabascan legend, the stories in this book remind us: we tell our stories to make sense of our experiences and to point the way to others. I hope this wonderful collection of first-person accounts (mostly written in 2014) will encourage you, regardless of age or gender, to think about how you want to live as you grow older. You'll meet some daring older women – like the mermaid sex goddess, monofin intact, gliding in the Caribbean; an early-sixties first-time bride finding her future husband on Craigslist; and a retired speech therapist starting a clinic in Cambodia. Fortunately, unlike the ancient Athabascans, we live in a time of longer lives and expanding opportunities for women although, obviously, many barriers persist.

In this book, you'll see women of different races, classes, and sexual orientations face various challenges and choices as they age. A loving daughter recounts how her mother moved beyond a "bare and unadorned" Mississippi upbringing. A California Chicana counters her mother's denial of her Mexican heritage. A bisexual polyamorist rejects a life like her mother's. There are (relatively) young elders – the writer/teacher/poet grappling with her legacy – and older ones – the nonagenarian New Englander investing (monetarily) in the future. And there are women who refuse to succumb to disabilities – like the retired history professor, with rheumatoid arthritis, now writing poetry. All are embracing new adventures and changing what it means to be an "older woman."

Taken together, however, these women do not represent the U.S. population. They are overwhelmingly white and middle-class. Many are highly educated; approximately half live in California. Yet, they begin to illustrate the diversity that characterizes the lives of older women, to offer insights into navigating the realities of age and gender, and to remind us that older women should be neither stereotyped nor ignored.

Given this cohort of women, you might be surprised that few of them mention the impact of feminism. As a retired professor of women's history, I was. Many of these authors participated in the second wave feminist movement during the late 1960s-1980s, and even women who never identified as feminists have been profoundly affected by the shifts in sex roles since the 1960s.

Why, I wondered, is there little or no mention of feminism? Clearly, some stories shun analysis. Others describe choices that have little to do with feminism. Some of the authors might view themselves as feminists but didn't see feminism as central to their stories. And, maybe, the changes caused by second-wave feminism are so deeply ingrained that most of these women never considered the connection between feminism and their present-day choices. As one friend argued in another context, "It isn't necessary to identify it [feminism as causal]; it's there, atmospheric, affecting everything, blowing open the doors we ventured through."

Do read about these women and enjoy their photos – including the performance artist embracing her theater dog, Fanny; the photographer laughing and dancing among women in Kenya; the American Indian/ Scottish writer hoisting her self-carved paddle after her first days-long canoe journey. Celebrate them! And let them inspire you despite those voices that still might challenge, *"You're Doing What?"*

Marjorie Penn Lasky,
Berkeley, California, 2017

Our stories can be enormously powerful, because they're about living, real human beings, not about theoretical descriptions in feminist literature.[2]
– Faye Wattleton,
"Twelve Quotes from Women that Will Inspire Activism"

Acknowledgements

As with any similar endeavor, this book exists only because of the contributions of numerous individuals, first and foremost the authors of these tales. In 2014, I began this project with an emailed invitation to friends and acquaintances. Word spread and, by the end of the year, I had received 135 narratives. The present authors, along with a separate group of writers whose stories appear on-line in a special edition of *History of Women in the Americas* seemingly maintained their good humor and willingness to answer my requests for rewrites and patience, as I handled personal crises and slowly slogged my way through the project. Thank you all! Thirty more narratives have yet to find their way onto a proposed website!

I am indebted to my wonderful editor, Kathy Gosnell, who submitted a narrative and then agreed to edit these stories. I don't know Kathy; I'm not even sure how she found me. I also don't know what I would have done without her.

Then there are the folks who graciously volunteered to edit, comment, or just hand-hold: Arlene Bernstein, Anita Goldstein, Susan Goldstein, Barbara Nube Roose, Agnes Riedmann, and Ruth Rosen. And, of course, Sharon Dirlam, whom I have yet to meet.

A special thanks to Nancy Rubin, photographer extraordinaire, whose photos of San Francisco Bay Area women appear here and in the on-line edition.

The computer skills and photographic prowess of my sister, Natec, are unmatched, and I can only thank her for her unflagging enthusiasm in responding to questions and problems, day and night!

A singular vote of appreciation goes to the editors of *History of Women in the Americas*, S. Jay Kleinberg, Sinead McEneaney, Helen Glew and Imaobong Umoren, for persevering in getting the forty-four other tales on-line. (See http://journals.sas.ac.uk/hwa/issue/view/348/showToc) And, of course, thanks to Rachel Ritchie.

I will be forever grateful to Naomi Brauner, the designer of this book's spectacular cover. Her taking control of its creation when I had no idea of what I wanted and her ability and patience in electronically holding my hand far exceeded my expectations. Carol Ehrlich suggested using the hands on the cover. And thanks to Mark Weiman of Regent Press for aiding and guiding me through the publication process.

This project probably wouldn't have occurred without "My Trip of Unintended Consequences" to Sedona. So kudos to the trip's initiators, my Wednesday Hiking Group that Eats Chocolate, and to the fearless (or was it fearful?) hiking leaders, Road Scholars' employees. Amazing what serendipity can occasion in one's life – regardless of age!

YOU'RE DOING *WHAT?*

We go through life. We shed our skins. We become ourselves.
— Patti Smith,
Details: The Music Issue, July 1993

COMPARING GENERATIONS

We are our ancestors... [We] fit into each other,
like these nesting cups.[3]

— SANDRA CISNEROS,
The House on Mango Street

Paola Gianturco

FOLLOWING IN MY MOTHER'S FOOTSTEPS

Different lives but an important maternal lesson.

Paola Gianturco and her mother, Verna Daily Gianturco, at home, 1942

At the age of 55, I decided to take a year off from my corporate life to create a coffee table book. I was not a professional photographer or writer so you might well think this was a harebrained scheme!

But I had done two jobs at the same time that year, which resulted in 1) a million frequent flier miles (so I could go – and stay – virtually anywhere free); 2) two years' worth of income, all earned in one year; 3) exhaustion. Time for a sabbatical!

I promised myself that for one year, I would do only what I loved most (photography and travel) and what I wanted to learn next (which was about women in the developing world). I had so much fun that I never went back to business.

Since then, I have photographed women's lives in 55 countries. To celebrate my seventy-fifth birthday this summer, I am starting my sixth photographic book.

During the past almost 20 years, much has changed in our world.

I've watched those changes in the most intimate, personal ways. Women invite me into their homes, introduce me to their children, sometimes we dance; sometimes they dress me up in their clothes.

But always, they tell me their hopes for their families and their communities. They have taught me something important: the answer to Sigmund Freud's question, "What does a woman want?" I know! Women want social, economic and political justice. They want health, education, a sustainable environment, equality and peace. The women in my books don't just dream about those goals, they organize into groups and work effectively to achieve them. Slowly, they are changing our world.

I feel fortunate to spend my time sitting on the floor in women's huts listening to their stories. Stories enough to fill five books. Stories enough to fill many speeches. Stories enough to inspire people to support these women's important work.

The women in my books have taught me to create a social, artistic and economic legacy. I give 100% of the author royalties from my books to nonprofit organizations working on the issues in the books. What I never imagined was that my philanthropy would inspire my readers' generosity and engagement. But I now know of hundreds of thousands of dollars that have been donated by readers to help women around the world. When I first discovered that, I wept. At the same time, I felt euphoric.

My mother's generation may not have pursued a second career. But it was my mother who taught me to pursue what I feel passionate about.

Mother worked as a bookkeeper before she got married and later, she became an enthusiastic member of a women's investment club. By the 1980s when the members were in their seventies, they cashed out. Their fund was modest, so their profits were relatively small. One woman bought a vacuum cleaner with her earnings.

Not my mother. She bought two airline tickets to San Francisco. My father was bemused that his wife was flying him across the country with her own money.

She had decided to see an exhibit of French Impressionist paintings – paintings that she loved beyond all telling. She went to the museum to see that exhibit four days in a row. Every day, she clamped on audio

Paola Gianturco, Kenya, 2006
(Photo by Norma Adhiambo)

tour earphones and enjoyed the very same narratives and the very same art. When I asked whether she felt four visits were excessive, she was astonished: "This is why I came! This is what I love!"

May we all find the reason we came – and be lucky enough to do what we love.

In 2013, author/photographer Paola Gianturco (74) was named one of "Forty Women to Watch Over Forty." In 2014, Women's eNews named her one of 21 Leaders for the 21ˢᵗ Century. Her book, Grandmother Power: A Global Phenomenon, *has won four gold awards including the International Book Award for Multicultural Nonfiction, and the 2012 Book of the Year Award for Women's Studies. One hundred percent of her author royalties from the book benefit grandmothers in 15 African countries who are raising children orphaned by AIDS. Her author website is www.paolagianturco.com.*

Mama exhorted her children at every opportunity to "jump at de sun." We might not land on the sun, but at least we would get off the ground.[4]
– ZORA NEALE HURSTON,
Dust Tracks on a Road

Rosemary Trimberger Lasche

REINVENTING MY POSSIBILITIES

How does a super-athlete's life differ from her mother's?

Being asked to write about becoming an older competing athlete was at first an amusing idea. I was born in 1945 and grew up long before women were allowed to run in marathons or even compete in most major organized sports. Women's role and identity were most often those of homemaker, not that of an athlete. My own mother was typical of this stereotype.

As an adult, I had always considered it important to stay in shape, to do various sports and activities, and to be outside enjoying the seasons. Pregnant with our son, I continued to play competitive games of squash with my husband, to roller skate around the McGill campus, and to swim with all the flat-bellied undergraduates. Later at Stanford I biked our son to day care and then biked to my job miles away, long before it was trendy to bike.

As the kids grew up, I was busy as a full-time working mom with a satisfying career as an administrator and therapist. But as I approached 50, I knew I needed to expand my life and my identity and so committed myself to race in the Boston Marathon. Having just turned 52 and on our eighteenth wedding anniversary, I ran my first race, the Boston Marathon. I was hooked! I had started experiencing another life ... a passion, a sense of purpose where my expectations became a focused determination and persistence.

I decided that I hadn't reached my athletic potential and that other athletic possibilities were within my reach. I had run a marathon to defy turning 50 and growing old, but it became more complicated and richer than that. My athletic pursuits have defined me, given me a different lifestyle, another priority, fostered a new mindset of competitiveness (against myself and others) and a belief in myself.

I did go on to run in 15 more marathons and decided just before I turned 60 that I wanted to do just one triathlon in my life. I chose the all-female Danskin Triathlon, whose motto proved prophetic, "The

woman who starts the race is not the same woman who finishes the race."
I continued to race in more triathlons and often came in first, second or
third in my age group, proving that I could hold my own as a triathlete.

In 2007, at age 62, I came in first in my age group in the Olympic
distance Cranberry Triathlon, but more noteworthy was that this was
the beginning of another new experience, that of being the oldest female athlete in a race. Since then it has happened multiple
times. I continue to have a need to push my physical and mental
limits by competing in seven or eight triathlons, half-marathons
and open water swim races each year. In August 2014, I placed
second in my division in the New York City Triathlon. Most
recently, in October 2015, after recovering from bicep tendon
surgery and to celebrate turning 70, I placed first in the Boston
Athletic Association Half-Marathon.

I love what training and racing tells me about myself, filling
my mind with planning, anticipation, satisfaction, excitement and
the necessity of mastering pre-race anxiety. I like the tiredness I
feel after hours of training and the glow after a race. And training
and racing are good for my marriage; my husband will tell you I
get irritable when I don't get enough exercise.

At first I laughed when thinking how my life as an older athlete is so different from my mother's. But in reality, it isn't. She had
endless energy and endurance as she skillfully and lovingly raised six
children while my Dad worked long hours to support us. She was not
one ever to be idle. I remember seeing her late at night after a long day,
designing and sewing beautiful clothes for her children. Even though
our ways of staying centered and relieving stress are different, I identify with that restless energy and drive to push myself. I realize now
that some of my mother's and my inner essence is the same although
the outward appearance may be very different.

*Rosemary Trimberger Lasche lives in the Boston area with her hus-
band and dog. Their lakefront cottage in Maine is a paradise for some
of her training and rejuvenation. Their daughter and son-in-law live
in Brooklyn and their son in San Francisco; they and where they live
expand Rosemary's world. In about a year, she plans on reinventing more
possibilities by not retiring but by recreating herself as an art student.*

Rosemary Trimberger Lasche's mother, Sally Trimberger, and her hand-crocheted tablecloth, Brookline, Massachusetts, 2009

Rosemary Trimberger Lasche, New York City, New York, 2014

Mom

Defining herself as Mexican, the author is unlike her mother

I am the dirty Mexican my mother never acknowledged but loved. Race. It is always hard to talk about and write about and to live. My mother was from a different era and a part of California with little racial or ethnic tolerance. Her world was smaller than today's world. She worked hard to shrink her world to a place she could feel safe. I don't know if she ever really felt safe. Isolated in a small mountain community, Mono Native Americans were the dominant minority, followed by a few Mexican families. We were one of the few.

Mom never claimed to be a Mexican. She would proudly state, "I am Spanish and French, not Mexican," so different from me and her other children. Dirty Mexicans. Yet she married twice, both Mexican men. It must have been very difficult for her to live her life knowing she had married a Mexican and had his children. Her closest friends, one my aunt, the other my *Madrina*, were both Mexican women. These women loved each other and would sit in the kitchen drinking coffee, smoking and laughing. Our family events all had Mexican roots. Yet, she always said, "I am Spanish and French, not Mexican." Always and forever. And I wonder, at times, what she thought of her daughter, of me.

My life is so different and although I shamefully admit to spending many years angry with my Mom, now that I am older, I find myself understanding her life a bit more. Notice I haven't said forgiving because, to me, *forgiving* speaks of a kind of arrogance. It's so Catholic. And, yes, forgiveness is so Mexican! Throughout my life I have found parts of my Mexican identity and savored each new finding as a precious artifact. Those very things my mother denied, I have embraced. The laundry list of differences isn't important to me, but the turning point in our mother/daughter relationship is.

Politics drove a permanent wedge between us. *Huelga!* In the farmworker strike, I found home. Marches, "shop-ins" and leafleting became a focal point in my life. Through the United Farmworkers Union (UFW), I found my way to a college campus. I found purpose and pride and I found understanding. I found my identity. I am Chicana, a being with Mexican roots, living in the United States, knowing the politics that have formed my identity. I found a life completely foreign to my mother and my family.

The readings and lectures in my Chicano Studies minor gave me understanding. California's history is one of racial unrest and, yes, injustice. My mother's choice to deny herself her heritage was about survival, both physical and psychological. Ironically, for years I ignored the fact that my father is only half Mexican. His father, my grandfather, came from India. Yes, I am my mother's daughter and like her, I endure … so Mexican!

All stories about our mothers are love stories… You may not find the love until the end of the story, or you may never find it. But others will.[5]

— BRANDON FRENCH,
"Forsaken"

Kathy Gosnell Seiler

A WOMAN IN THE MIDDLE

The author as a bridge between her mother and daughter

We are on a continuum, my mother, my daughter and I. Mom embraced Catholicism. She married once and forever. She was a stay-at-home mom who, armed with a high school diploma and a love of reading, started working part-time at the local public library when the youngest of her five children started kindergarten. She retired 16 years later as the head librarian.

I agonized for years and ultimately severed myself from religion. Mom and Dad were not enthusiastic about my going to college, but there was a state university in our town, so I went, living at home and working part-time. My parents did not want me to study journalism, a profession then dominated by men, but I prevailed and spent most of my career as a newspaper copy editor.

My daughter, a fraternal twin, grew up with no religious affiliation but with a powerful moral code. College was assumed, and she attended a fine one on the East Coast, far from our California home. She then served in the Peace Corps and recently started work on a master's degree in public health.

My children, the twins, were born when I was 40 and married to my third husband. My son died of complications of cerebral palsy before his second birthday, and that marriage ended in divorce, as had the first two.

Until the stock market crashed in 1929 and the country plunged into the Great Depression, my mother's family was relatively affluent. She finished high school, but some of her younger sisters did not because they had to work.

The family in which I grew up had no money for extras. I have early memories of eating French toast or cereal for supper. On my 16th birthday I started a part-time job and my parents told me they could no longer pay for my clothes, books and other expenses.

Mom never lived alone. She was the oldest of six and was living in her parents' home and working in Manhattan when she met Dad, who was in the Army Air Forces. They married in 1944 and went to a base in Georgia. She moved back to New York, pregnant with me, when he went overseas. After the war, they moved to a small town in Illinois. Dad died there in 2001, and after that Mom shared her home with at least one of her sons until dementia dictated a move to a retirement home. She died in 2005.

Choosing dense urban areas because of my work, I have lived alone for many years, before and between marriages and after my daughter left for college 13 years ago. My daughter has lived in this country's three largest cities and in a hut in West Africa.

In recent years, I have often been a volunteer, particularly in educational programs. I was provisionally accepted in the Peace Corps in 2011 and would have gone to Eastern Europe or Central Asia as a teacher. Instead, I failed the medical exam and continued my newspaper work. I applied again and failed again in 2014. My daughter has done community service work since she was in elementary school, and her decision to join the Peace Corps seemed as natural as breathing.

How do I compare to my mother? She married happily; I married often. She finished high school; I finished college. She raised five children; I raised one. She worked outside her home for 16 years; I worked outside my home full-time for 45 years. She helped people find great books to read; I helped reporters express themselves as writers. Now I give time to strangers; Mom mostly gave her time to family and home. Mom was either braver or more stoic than I am: No matter how much fear or pain she felt, no matter what regrets she had, I never saw her cry. My daughter cannot say that.

I am the bridge between these two strong women.

Kathy Gosnell Seiler is retired and living again in the Illinois town where she grew up. She volunteers and works whenever she can as a freelance copy editor.

**Kathy Gosnell Seiler,
Pasadena, California, 2009**

Rose Dosti
MY PERSONAL ODYSSEY

Political and economic changes lead to generational differences

My mother's generation probably would not be doing what I do. Not that it couldn't. Different political and economic factors defined their world – the Great Depression, WWI and WWII, and the awakening but not yet blossoming socio/economic freedoms for women. The economic, political and social factors that define my life's work differ markedly. In fact, I would not be writing this if I were not the daughter of immigrant parents from Albania and married to a political émigré whose seven siblings had been imprisoned under the communist regime for 47 years. Their imprisonment occurred during a political cleansing that lasted until 1991, when communism throughout Eastern Europe finally collapsed.

My mother, married to a man twice her age whom she hardly knew, immigrated to New York's Lower East Side in 1929. She knew no English. She had no profession. She knew little about the culture or complexities of living in the most progressive country in the world. Yet, she heroically mastered a life of hard work, determination and vision and gave my sister, Mary, and me the tools to take advantage of the opportunities that the United States offered. Were it not for my mother's vision and sacrifice, my sister and I would not have been exposed at an early age to the arts – music, dance, theater and writing – or pursued other goals. My passions were my life.

Rose Dosti's mother, Farfuri
Lilaj Rushit, Boston,
Massachusetts, 2001

My sister, Mary, won scholarships first to Harvard/Radcliff to study anthropology and then to Smith for a master's degree in child development. She later taught at several universities and eventually served as community representative with the Massachusetts Office for Children. Today she advocates avidly for justice.

After I married Luan Dosti, a home fire destroyed all hope of economic stability for our family of five, including a 6-week old newborn. My husband and I abandoned our desires to further our education and entered the workplace. I became a food critic and lifestylewriter for the *Los Angeles Times* for 35 years. Upon retirement, I taught journalism until the sudden and unexpected collapse of communism changed everything.

In 1991 my husband reunited with his seven long-lost siblings in Albania who, like tens of thousands of other Albanian citizens, suffered political imprisonment under Enver Hoxha's brutal dictatorship. Meeting my husband's siblings and hearing their stories shocked and moved me into new directions. Who in the world knew about Albania's tragic history during the Cold War? How could Albania's secret calamity in the midst of Western neighbors be exposed honorably?

Precisely at this point, age 75, I experienced an unexpected spiritual transformation and converted to Christianity. These events guided me toward a life of service in Albania as a missionary in service of the Lord.

A Fulbright grant in 2004 enabled me, with the help of my sister and other like-minded human rights advocates, to produce a short documentary film "Prison Nation," in order to expose the truth about survivors of Albania's Cold War period. In 2008 the group founded the Albanian Human Rights Project (AHRP) dedicated to filming and preserving testimonies of former Albanian political prisoners under the communist regime (1944-1991) as historical documents for scholarly study, education, and inspiration, now and in the future.

To interview and film survivors willing to tell their stories, I needed to live in Albania periodically for six months. So far, AHRP has filmed 100 testimonies, averaging 1½ hours each, which are being curated and preserved at the Wende Museum of the Cold War in Culver City, California and at the University of Southern California Digital Repository, where they are accessible for scholarly study.

I was shocked by the brutality of the survivors' stories and the impact on their lives even today, as many continue to be marginalized citizens. Yet I was also stunned by their lack of bitterness toward their tormentors. "How can that be?" I asked. Their lives testify to the triumph of the human spirit, a profound lesson for any privileged American.

The project is finished, although fundraising to pay for English translations continues. Only when it is completed will the AHRP gift the collection to the Wende Museum.

My other work involves teaching at Santa Monica College's Emeritus program and continuing my life-long passions – writing, painting, drawing, sculpting and music. Then there are the joys of having three wonderful children – Lisa, Marya and Ben – and four grandchildren – Christina, Ryan, Gideon and Luke. What more can one ask?

If the political and economic issues that defined my mother's generation had differed, would a woman of that age group have done as I do? Of course she would.

Information about the Albanian Human Rights Project (AHRP) and two short documentary films, *"Prison Nation: Albania 1944-1991"* and *"Lost Voices Making History"* is available at www.albanianhumanrightsproject.org.

Rose Dosti has been a missionary in Albania since 2006. She is the author of eight books on food and is a two-time Fulbright Scholar and Specialist teaching journalism and English conversation for advanced speakers at the Lincoln Center Tirana in Albania since 2004. As a missionary, Rose has hosted ongoing Bible studies for men and women in Albania, where 75% of the population declares no religious affiliation. Rose, who lives in southern California, is featured in Who's Who of American Women.

Rose Dosti receiving the keys to the city of Tirana, Albania from Mayor Erion Veliaj for work on the Albanian Human Rights Project, 2016

Van Pham

A SHORT STORY ABOUT A LITTLE VIETNAMESE LADY

Ngan Vu, the author's mother, breaks with tradition

Ngan Vu was born in May 1935 in Kien An, an urban area of District Hai Phong, northern Vietnam. She grew up in a very traditional and conservative family with three siblings and six half brothers and half sisters. Her loving father had high status in the society. Her mother was a traditional Vietnamese lady who held traditional virtues by dutifully following many Vietnamese traditions, such as chewing betel, dying her teeth black, and wearing only traditional outfits. Her father had four wives (polygamy was legal and common in Vietnam during those days). Although Ngan admires many of her Vietnamese customs and traditions, she often wonders how her father was able to manage conflicts among his wives. Most of all, she is thankful that she did not have to be a part of a polygynous union.

Since the French had colonized Vietnam in the mid-1850s, Vietnamese culture was also influenced and westernized by the early 20th century. It was evident that traditional values were blended with Western trends by this time. Most of the social changes were much criticized. Women who followed the changes were considered to be of easy virtue. Conflicts escalated between the older generation and the younger one, the foreign and the traditional, the urban and the rural. Growing up in such a transitional society, Ngan, like many others of the younger generation, was more open-minded and welcomed some of the social transformations. She preferred wide-legged pants and modern *áo dài* (Vietnamese national tunic dress) over the conventional skirts, traditional outfits (*áo dài* or *áo tứ thân*) her mom always wore. She preferred the fashionable European hair styles (hair perming or letting it down) over the traditional hair style (winding the hair with a cloth string to form a small pony tail arranged on one side of the head).

Ngan did not like betel chewing. This thousand-year-old Vietnamese custom involves folding betel leaves in different ways and

Ngan Vu, 3rd from left, and Van Pham, 2nd from right, 2013

wrapping a piece of dry areca nut inside. Betel leaves and areca nuts are symbols of love and marriage in the Vietnamese society. They are two of the most essential items that must be present in every wedding ceremony. Chewing the mixture is also a good remedy against bad breath. However, Ngan could never tolerate the distinct flavor of the mixture. She also found it unattractive and amusing to have red-stained lips.

Another Vietnamese tradition Ngan did not follow as her mother did was tooth-blackening. Although this custom is often misunderstood as the result of betel chewing (which would convey only stains of brownish color), tooth-blackening is instead the result of a ritual, a deliberate lacquering process.

In the 1900s, having lacquered teeth was a sign of beauty and a tooth-decay preventive. There were also strong cultural and religious beliefs that long, white teeth belong to demons and animals. However, the process of blackening teeth is not an easy one and somewhat painful due to the ingredients that are used to rinse and sanitize the mouth (lemon juice, fish sauce and saline solution) and to make the dye (potato plant and shellac).

Ngan still remembers watching her older cousins and her old-est sister enduring the pain during the process. It scared her so much that she decided never to dye her teeth black. Fortunately, her family migrated to South Vietnam in 1954 where tooth blackening is much less common. She was able keep her white and beautiful teeth.

In 1954, after the end of the First Indochina War, Ngan's father knew they would not be safe in communist North Vietnam. He decided to migrate with his family to the South through Operation Passage to Freedom. They built new roots in Saigon. Ngan got married on November 22, 1963. She and her husband had five children (two sons and three daughters). After the fall of Saigon in April 1975, life proved to be very difficult. Ngan's husband and their sons joined the two million boat people and fled Vietnam in 1979. After spending a year at a refugee camp in Indonesia, they arrived in the United States. After settling in Southern California and as soon as he could, Ngan's husband registered his wife and daughters, who still were in Saigon, with the Orderly Departure Program. In May 1986, after seven years apart, their family was reunited. Today, Ngan and her husband have 10 grandchildren and live in Huntington Beach, California. Van Pham is one of their daughters.

The more a daughter knows the details of her mother's life...
the stronger the daughter.[6]

— ANITA DIAMANT,
The Red Tent

Kathy Labriola

BERKELEY IS A LONG WAY FROM NEW JERSEY (OR) THIS APPLE FELL PRETTY FAR FROM THE TREE

Making sure not to live like her mother

I was born in 1954 in New Jersey. My mother was the quintessential working-class wife and mother who lived through hell for 30 years in an abusive marriage. Married at 19, a virgin, she had five children by the time she was 26. My father was a minister who was often fired for having sex with married women parishioners. Each time, the church hushed it up and gave him another church in a different county.

My mother was a devout Christian who believed she should accept any abuse. She was saddled with children and no way to support them. After the last child left home, however, she became a registered nurse and filed for divorce when she got her first job. She later married a man who treated her like a queen, and she had 15 years of happiness until he died.

As a child, I knew my mother was trapped. I became convinced that marriage and motherhood were the culprits, and I was acutely aware that my siblings and I were the chains my father used to hold her hostage. Not until I was an adult could I see the more complex reality, how sexism and poverty also caused her oppression.

My foremost goals were to be single and childless to avoid my mother's fate. A marketable skill was essential, so I trained as a licensed vocational nurse at the local hospital. I graduated at 19 and fled to a feminist commune in Berkeley, California. I had my ticket to a good-paying job, and for 25 years it supported me well. Having watched my parents struggle financially, I considered it a luxury to have a job that paid the rent, bought health insurance, and provided such pleasures as going to Grateful Dead concerts and donating to political causes. Frugal living allowed me to work three to four days a week and be a union shop steward and political activist. Not to mention drugs, sex, and rock and roll; it was the '70s, after all.

I worked in a nursing home, in a respiratory intensive care unit, as a nurse in AIDS research, and as a home healthcare nurse helping severely disabled infants. I found the work satisfying, but it was clear to me that nursing was not a perfect fit. I began to see my role as protecting patients from the medical system, and I struggled with mixed feelings about the dehumanizing way healthcare was delivered.

In 1992, I trained in hypnotherapy and opened a practice as a nurse, counselor, and hypnotherapist. I seek to provide compassionate affordable counseling for people who are not well served by our mental health system, LGBT clients, drug addicts, sex workers, and people with depression and anxiety.

Because I have a history of being in an open relationship, many struggling with this issue come to me for counseling. I have never hidden my non-monogamous life. People who were desperate for information and tools to manage this very challenging relationship style found very little written information. So I wrote articles on open relationships and photocopied them as free pamphlets. A small publishing company published my first book about open relationships in 2010.

I'm happy with my life as an unmarried childless woman. I am part of the first generation of women to have access to safe, reliable birth control, good-paying jobs and the cultural permission to live independently. Control over my body and access to decent-paying work have allowed me to create a career, engage in political activism, write books, and build intimate relationships and community.

I am a godparent and an aunt, and I enjoy being a part of the lives of a few beloved children. However, I believe motherhood is a calling, and I know that it is not mine. Not spending the prime of my life raising children has given me opportunities for fulfillment and happiness that my mother could not imagine. Feminism's true gift has been to give women options. I have utmost respect for the choices each woman makes and ask only that others respect mine.

Kathy Labriola is a nurse, counselor, and hypnotherapist in private practice in Berkeley, California, providing affordable mental health services to alternative communities. She has been a card-carrying bisexual and polyamorist for more than 40 years. She has written and published Love in Abundance: A Counselor's Advice on Open Relationships *and* The Jealousy Workbook. *She is extra crunchy and lives in a housing co-op, rides a bike, and raises chickens and organic vegetables. Her website is www.kathylabriola.com.*

Kathy Labriola's (pregnant) mother, Patricia Binder, Kathy's brother, Les Labriola on left and Kathy, New Jersey, 1956

Kathy Labriola at home, 2014

Hellena Jones Elbling

THE ORIGINAL D.I.V.A.: A DETERMINED INDIVIDUAL WITH VALUES AND ASSETS

The author's mother as an inspiration

The journey to becoming a certified life coach was an eye-opening experience. It helped me to see the true value of others and to accept that the person taking me for granted the most was me. To honor myself and other women, I created the acronym D.I.V.A., which stands for Determined Individual with Values and Assets. It amazes me how this acronym changed the way I look at myself and other women. D.I.V.A. gives me permission to celebrate my triumphs and challenges and to create strategies for success.

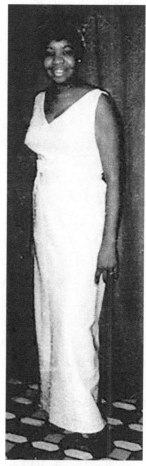

Hellena Jones Elbling's mother, Helen Stephen Jones, 1965

My mother was my D.I.V.A. blueprint. She was strong and true; nothing got past her. She was not what you'd call an overly affectionate woman. I think growing up in Macon, Georgia, and being the oldest girl of 11 brothers and sisters tuckered her out. Still, she showed my siblings and me love in her way. Looking back, now I believe that was best; it kept her emotions honest.

Growing up in the South during the 1930s and '40s made many African American women scared of their own shadows. For my mom, it was the opposite. She was only 21 when she became a widow with three young boys. Instead of living that life, she made her way to Washington, D.C., and never looked back. She met my father soon after and started a courtship that resulted in me, their love child, and then marriage. She was determined to prove to herself and especially to my grandmother that she was more than her color or sex presumed her to be. What that was she didn't know, but she was going to find out.

My mom was the quintessential fashionista of her day. She was naturally graceful and regal, which made everything she wore just right. I

Hellena Jones Elbling, 2014

loved it when she and my father dressed for cabarets. She wore long sequined gowns and pinned her hair atop her head like a crown. She wasn't afraid to express her individuality and her desire to be different. I often wonder where she developed such strength to strike out on her own. I believe her desire for a better life was stronger than the option of accepting her current situation. As a young girl, I wanted to fit in. My mother, however, never missed an opportunity to model what it meant to be an individual and to hold her head high.

The epitome of my mother honoring her values was demonstrated when she received a raise – on the spot. She'd been working part-time in the women's outerwear department of a major retail chain and became a top seller. Not waiting for recognition, she made an appointment with her manager and told him exactly why he needed to raise her salary. After reviewing her facts and noting the department's revenue increase, he gave her what she wanted. What I love about her story is that she gathered her evidence before walking into his office. There was no pleading, hesitation or emotion leading the conversation, just a woman knowing her value and standing up for it.

On March 1, 2006, eight years after her death, I had an epiphany regarding my mother: I realized this women was an entrepreneur.

Growing up, it never dawned on me that a person could work for herself. She used all of her assets and talents to create her entrepreneurial opportunities. Her first passion was making other women feel and look beautiful. She became a licensed beautician and earned a degree in business management to run her own business. Her love of makeup led to her position as an Avon representative. Her passion for fashion helped her become the best saleswomen in her department store. And later in life, just for fun, she used her keen sense of direction to take a job as a cab driver. She excelled in each of her endeavors because she matched her assets to the tasks at hand. Mom gave me a wonderful blueprint to follow to match passion with skill. I see every woman as a D.I.V.A., and I coach from that perspective, encouraging each woman's greatness from within.

I never truly understood the lessons my mom was trying to teach me until I became a D.I.V.A., loving and honoring myself and respecting my skills and talents. As a personal and business coach, the most important lesson I teach my clients is this: "Until you know what your strengths and values are, no one else will."

Hellena Jones Elbling is a certified professional co-active coach who studied at the Coaches Training Institute in San Rafael, California, and holds a bachelor's degree in human services management from the University of Phoenix. Her jewelry line, Creations by Hellena, allows her to create jewelry that represents empowering qualities. She lives in Venice, California with her husband, Peter, and their cat, Jonesy. Her website is www.coreilluminations.com.

For we think back through our mothers if we are women.[7]
— VIRGINIA WOOLF,
A Room of One's Own

Shelley Holstein

THE ART OF LIVING IN THE LAYERS
(ACKNOWLEDGING STANLEY KUNITZ'S "THE LAYERS")

*The author connects her creativity to her
mother's muted ingenuity*

**Shelley Holstein's mother,
Charlotte Wolk, and Shelley,
Pittsburgh, Pennsylvania, 1948**

To introduce myself, I am a retired psychotherapist who spent more than half of my life living in the complex and often painful lives of others, abandoning my own, except for a few stolen moments which I devoted to playing the violin. My retirement goal, of course, was to play music as much as possible. I raised two amazing and very successful children and helped raise two incredibly talented, devoted, equally successful stepchildren. I now have seven adorable grandchildren.

When I was struck with a form of arthritis, somewhere on the continuum between osteoarthritis and rheumatoid, I found that little by little I had to give up most of my small life's pleasures and keep reinventing myself to avoid, I suppose, killing myself. When my knees went, I had to give up taking long walks with good friends, when my shoulder went, it was golf, but the most devastating blow came when it reached my hands and I could no longer play the violin. The important and obvious lesson here: Don't wait until retirement to follow your dreams. Then my hearing started to fail, which made even listening to great music a challenge. So I turned to painting watercolors. I have little natural talent, but with hard work I can turn out some fairly decent work, which I find pleasing and rewarding. Most recently I have begun to write poetry. I certainly am in the infant stage of understanding what makes great poetry, but to date, I'm enjoying the process.

I attribute my strength of perseverance and love of creativity to my mother, who was a talented and varied artist in sumi-ink paintings, marble sculpture and jewelry making. She was a brilliant woman and a startling example of the feminist ideal long before it was a movement! I, however, understand that about her only now, now that she's gone. For most of my life I saw only her surface self, the one she created to survive in an age when women were valued only for the sacrifices they made on behalf of their families.

I never fully understood the mostly hidden and complex layers of her being. I have never surpassed my mother but do continue the struggle to greet her strength of character and creativity.

Perhaps the following poem reflects the unfolding of my understanding:

ROOTS AND BRANCHES

I. Long after you were gone
    I found a an old frayed folio in the
        Back of the closet,
            hidden,
                forgotten.
    A tiny blue bird
        amidst cherry blossoms peered out
            and into the tangle of my thoughts.
    With a single breath
        you had painted a strong, graceful branch!
    With a meditative sigh,

a splash of delicate blossoms-
Leaves, suspended, mysteriously
floating.
I was silenced
against all my judgment of you.
For all those years
Blinded by your bigotry,
your domineering and condescending
manner,
your surface shadow self.
I had turned away never knowing
how many layers upon layers
of your fiber lay hidden.
Why hidden?
Was sacrifice all that was honored?
For what did you have to atone?
Please come back and tell me who you were.

II. Long after you were gone
Your strong, unyielding branches
continued to extend and ensnare
my entire universe.
When you were felled,
my shallow roots crumbled as well.
I feared crossing bridges,
vast, open spaces,
the critical voice of the night,
and dark silence.
I immersed myself in the lives of others seeking
asylum,
looking for power,
looking for answers.
And I planted a small spindly Redwood in the
corner of my garden.
And it grew tall,
with new feathery branches,

And it grew strong,
    a warm house for living creatures.
And it grew and it grew.

If you do come back will you recognize who I am.

Shelley Holstein was born in Pittsburgh, Pennsylvania, which accounts for her great sense of humor, and now lives in Eureka, California, where she's happy to report that it's no longer necessary to have a large truck with a gun rack and a black dog in the back. She lives with her husband of 40 years (the marriage not her husband). She paints and is just short of calling herself an artist, writes poetry, reads voraciously (anything that isn't a professional book) and travels extensively, mostly to visit her children and grandchildren, as nobody wants to come to Eureka.

Shelley Holstein at home, 2014

Natec A.K.A. Linda Penn
A LONG, STRANGE TRIP...

A life substantially different from her mother's (and father's)

Natec and the swami of the mountain, India, 2010

Born in 1947, I was part of the ignition switch of the big boom that was to follow. In keeping with many of my generation, my life has differed greatly from those of my parents'. I became a radical political activist when I was 15 years old, which put me at odds with them. My marches with Reverend King for voting rights and against the war in Vietnam were a source of loud dinner confrontations, as the generation gap between us became a sprawling canyon. Over the rest of my parents' lives the gap existed, though fortunately the birth of my son and our subsequent visits helped us find ways to set animosity aside and share our love.

At 67, I am physically active, as were my parents at my age. Both were avid golfers; Dad got a hole in one at age 70 and Mom played into her late seventies. She was proud of the daily two-mile walks she took well into her eighties. At age 50, Mom became a travel agent and traveled the world in tour groups.

I, however, played one round of golf when I was 16 and never played again, thus proving that playing golf is not a genetic trait. And I, too, have traveled throughout the world, though never with a tour group.

I lived in the Haight-Ashbury in my early twenties, in the California wilderness in my late twenties, and in India for three years in my thirties. I migrated between western Canada and the tip of Baja with my commune family into my forties. Then when I was 41, when my son was less than a year, I moved to Hawai'i and my life became more conventional. Over the next 17 years, I became a single mom driving my son to school and to his soccer games, living in a house with indoor plumbing.

In 2009, at age 62, I had the opportunity to return to India through a chance meeting with a spiritual teacher who invited me to video-tape his annual group pilgrimage. I had given up on the notion of a monotheistic god and the Judeo-Christian creation myth back in my twenties. Animism and Eastern mythologies and philosophies made more sense to me. Organized religions were not appealing, but I res-onated with the trappings of Buddhism and Hinduism. The furnish-ings, art, and music in my homes always reflected this. I delved deeply into Tibetan Buddhist practices and Hindu (mainly Shivite) teachings. Returning to India was a great blessing.

I have been going back to India every year since. I trudge up moun-tainside paths to sit in caves to meditate. I walk nine miles around the base of Mt. Arunachala, a holy mountain, several times over my month-long stays. Sometimes I do it alone, sometimes with a half a million other people during the full moon. I eat food from street vendors (but unlike in my thirties I check with other Westerners to see if their stom-achs survived the experience). I relish the presence of being, the open looking into a stranger's eyes (so like when I lived in the Haight in its heyday), the simplicity of life. I meet the heartbreak of the pervasive poverty and illness with a prayer on my lips and a deepening love.

My parents lived in an apartment (albeit a large one) in a city for forty years. My home in Hawai'i is a little farm with three dogs, five cats, 14 ducks (and many ducklings), six hens, tropical fruit trees, and a long sight line into the adjoining state forest. My lifestyle includes weeding the land, doing farm chores and enjoying sitting in a field doing nothing but looking at the sky or watching the animals play.

Unlike my parents, I'm not retired. I will probably keep working making videos and teaching videography until I can't. And I'll just keep on keepin' on, blessed with good health and a strong body (albeit that dang right knee), an intelligence that wants to keep on learning, and a mindfulness that allows me to let it all go.

Peace out

Natec lives on the Big Island of Hawai'i. She just had the best Mother's Day, walking along the ocean cliffs with her son, Kawa, and the dogs. And then eating the tastiest coconuts and tropical fruit from her blessed little farm.

Natec, her parents, Sylvia and Sam Penn, and Natec's son, Kawa, Palm Springs, California, 1991

FAMILY
REDEFINED

We have three kinds of family
1. Those we are born to
2. Those who are born to us
3. And those we let into our hearts[8]

— SHERRILYN KENYON,
Winter's Night

Effie Hall Dilworth

LOST FAMILY FOUND

At 68, the author discovers her father was a paper son

Effie Hall and Pop, Yee Yung Lung, 1949

The year I was 68 years old, I learned these things about my father: he had two younger sisters, one of whom is still alive, living in Hong Kong; this sister has three sons, one in Cupertino, an hour away from me, the other two in Hong Kong; he had an older half brother who had two children; he had a younger half brother whom he never met, who has two children; all of them live in Guangzhou, China; he had 25 cousins, the children of his father's three brothers and one sister; his father was married three times; my father and his sisters were the children of the second wife.

* * *

Pop, as my sibs and I called our father, told me that he came from China by himself as a young boy and lived with an uncle in Needles, California, until he graduated from high school.

One uncle. Not a word about parents, brothers, sisters.

* * *

It is a year later now. I have been to Hong Kong, Guangzhou, Cupertino and Los Angeles and have met the children of my father's sister – my first cousins; met the uncle who was the younger of my father's two half brothers, and his children who are technically my half first cousins. (Our grandfathers are one and the same, but my grandmother was his second wife while their grandmother was his first wife.) The grandson of my father's older half-brother (progeny of my grandfather's first wife) and I have become comrades in our efforts to fill in the blanks about our fathers' family.

It is an amazing thing to discover the existence of aunts, uncles, and cousins – closely related kin – when you've lived so long thinking your father was nearly an orphan. My first step was a phone call to a man living in Needles who might possibly be a relative. Indeed, he was a distant cousin. Then I spoke to his older sister. From there I met, by telephone, the cousin who had been amassing family stories and pictures for the last eight years, beginning with his father's reminiscences.

I was not a child when my father died: I was 21 and he was 58. But my memories of him focused on his having been a loving, understanding parent. Now I aimed to learn whatever I could about him, about his background. What did his extended family know about him? As it turns out, not much. They'd heard that they had a relative in San Francisco who'd started a soy sauce factory. Only one uncle I spoke to had ever met him.

So over the course of this year, I learned quite a bit about my father's people if not a lot about my father. But a larger theme has emerged: clan, blood, family. I didn't expect to be turning over these notions at this point in my life. My siblings, my father, my mother and her siblings, their children – that was family that did not bear thinking about; they were ingrained in my childhood. But my ready acceptance of people I'd met so recently, the familiarity I felt simply because they were identified as "family" – this mystifies me. And the strength of such a bond, even when it is just the thickness of a thread, astonishes me.

* * *

My father, Yee Yung Lung, was born in 1908 in a village in Canton, China. When he was 12, his parents bought a paper from a

Chinese-American citizen named Hom Hong documenting the existence of a 10-year old son named Hom Hall. My father assumed the identity of this boy and came to America with Mr. Hom in 1921; he was now presumed to be a citizen of the United States. After a brief stay with Mr. Hom's family in Arizona, Hom Hall joined his uncle in Needles.

Hom Hall took the name George Hom Hall soon after his arrival in this country. This was my father's American identity. My parents deliberately created the silence around the subject of his family to hide the fact that he had entered the country illegally. The possibility of being deported, were this discovered, shadowed him until the last three months of his life, when he received a green card.

Effie Hall Dilworth graduated from U.C. Berkeley in English literature. She worked for the university for 30 years with the campus' natural history collections as a computer programmer and the administrator of a database system. She is the mother of two boys and has three grandchildren. In June 2013, the Chinese Historical Society of America published a booklet her cousin, Connie Young Yu, and she wrote about the family soy sauce enterprise, "Wing Nien Brand, A Story of Longevity."

Effie Hall Dilworth, Berkeley, California, 2014

Jacqueline Hackel

JACQUELINE ET MAMAM

The author's life was an enigma to her mother

**Jacqueline Hackel, her husband, David Rubsamen, and her mother,
Shelly Mandelbaum, Emeryville, California, 1996**

In memory my mother is seated at my dining room table, her gray hair carefully styled and sprayed into place. Her elegant but no longer fashionable jacket is draped over her shoulders revealing a pearl and gold pin on the collar. She wears a string of pearls, single pearl earrings, and the five-caret canary diamond ring she inherited from her mother, which rests uneasily on her small hand. The dutiful daughter of Victorian parents, she has no interest in modern fashion, although she loves clothes. She is looking around at the friends my husband and I have invited to dinner. I propose a toast "to family, and to friends who are family too." She has known everyone for many years and yet I see an expression cross her face that I cannot decipher. "Jacqueline," she says in her French-inflected English, revealing her native language "that is so B Zaar."

Everyone laughs, but I feel sad that she cannot understand why I would refer to the two men at the table as family. She cannot understand that I remain friends with men who twenty-five years earlier were my lovers. When I met the man who was to become my second husband, I told him I came as a package ... in addition to my son and daughter, I had two male friends from our time in graduate school. I considered us a "family of choice." I asked him if he could accept us all. They too were my history. We were inextricably intertwined. None of us saw the need to exile one another from our lives. We did not want to lose our own histories. In each case when being partners had proved untenable, we worked to transform the bond into a lasting friendship.

My husband met the challenge, in time creating a connection to each man.

Sent into an arranged marriage at 17, my mother never knew another man besides my father. She was deeply attached to her brothers yet she could not conceive of the category "former boyfriend, now friend." She never had to ask herself if there was a role for a man beyond father, brother, husband, son. She did not have the history that would raise the question. She was puzzled by my enduring attachments and stunned when one of the men invited the three of us to dinner with his lady friend. The structure of my social world was alien to her.

My mother's world was defined by the parameters of our family. She never would have gone into a restaurant alone, taken a trip without my father or pursued a college degree, although she spoke four languages. My lifestyle was a puzzlement and a worry to her. That I was single for 25 years between marriages was outside her framework of understanding. How could a woman with children live like this?

Differences between mothers and daughters are common enough. In our case it was an entire worldview. What I wanted for myself she could not understand: I wanted to be single. I did not want to remarry. I wanted to return to the university and obtain my doctorate. I wanted to travel to exotic places. I wanted adventures. None of these choices was ever on my mother's wish list. My life was an enigma to her. That I managed without a husband struck her as amazing. That my children could thrive without a man in the house was a revelation. That I had men friends however was the step she could not take ... she simply did not believe it. Her daughter's very modern "family" was a "B zaar" aberration.

That I succeeded in creating this complex family was due in no small part to the wider culture which permitted broad definitions of "family," thus I had the support my mother could not give. Had my mother attempted friendship with a man, her community would have closed ranks against her. No doubt my father would have felt cuckolded. No such issue arose for my husband.

They are all dead now ... my mother, my husband, my two friends. The void is excruciating.

Jacqueline Hackel, PhD, a clinical psychologist, has flown more than a million miles, enjoying exotic adventures. She is particularly proud of climbing Mount Kilimanjaro. When she isn't working, she is planning her next trip.

Jacqueline Hackel, Borneo, 2017

E. Kay Trimberger

A DIFFERENT KIND OF FAMILY

A single mother adopts a mixed-race baby

My mother had difficulty accepting that her daughter at age 40, a single professional woman, adopted a five-day-old mixed-race baby boy. She held onto the traditional view that a woman had either a career or a family, certainly not both if you were single. An interracial family was also beyond her understanding, although she and the rest of my family became very accepting of the charming, handsome child that my son became. Given these qualms, adoption seemed unproblematic, the morally preferable way for a single woman to become a parent. Both she and I believed that nurture was determinative. I believed that one could bring any baby from any class, race or location in the world into a family and, if treated equivalently, the child would grow up to be no different from a biological child. My mother was not surprised that in my private adoption, I got information about both his birth parents, as I explained that someday my son might want to find them for medical reasons or to satisfy some curiosity. But this would not concern our family.

My mother in her mid-seventies exalted in being a grandparent to five biological grandchildren and to my adopted one. She could not have imagined that in my seventies I would have no grandchildren but that my family would include a wide array of members of my son's birth families in Louisiana, relatives on both his black father's and white mother's side, including other mixed-race half-siblings of my son.

Being a single parent was not easy, nor was crossing race and class barriers as part of being an interracial family, but it was adoption that has challenged me the most and where my experience has most changed my ideas. Only after I helped my son at age twenty-six find his birth families, all of whom were very accepting of him, did I come to understand those aspects of him, both talents and problems, that make him so different from anyone else in my family. Only then did I understand how important a genetic and prenatal heritage is, not just for physical characteristics of a person, but also for interests and personality. But this was very late in his life and in mine. I now know that I could have been a better parent, and could better have helped my son navigate the pitfalls of adolescence, if I had known his birth heritage and if he could have known more about it too.

If the adoption had been opened sooner, while he was growing up, both he and I could have had a biological and an adopted family, different for each of us but bringing a symmetry into our family life. My biological family was his adoptive one; his biological family could have been my adoptive one. Today, my son doesn't fit comfortably into either family, not the one in which he grew up or the one with whom he shares a biological heritage.

As in any large extended family, both my son and I are closer to some of his relatives than to others. Although I am white, both of us have closer ties to the father's black family, me to his wife (no biological relation to either of us) and my son to his half-sister, his father's daughter. A few months ago, the stepmother called me to tell me that my son had been taken to a hospital in Oakland. He had sent a text to his sister in a southern state, but he, out of embarrassment, had not yet told me. This is how family should work.

I would have thought I would be closer to the white family, which is more like mine in social class and religion, but guilt undermines our closeness – the birth mother's and my guilt that in distinct ways we enabled our son's substance abuse.

When anyone asks me now whether they should adopt, I reply, "Yes, if you want to be a pioneer in forging a new kind of extended family, linking biological and adoptive relatives with your adopted child as the center of a network that comprises a complex kind of new family."

E. Kay Trimberger, a sociologist, is professor emerita at Sonoma State University. She is writing a book tentatively titled Creole Son: An Adoptive Mother's Story of Nurture and Nature. *She blogs occasionally on* The Huffington Post *and* Psychology Today. *Her website is https://ekaytrimberger.com.*

E. K. Trimberger at home, 2014
(Photo by Nancy Rubin)

E. Kay's son, Marco, and his father, Robert, Louisiana, 2010
(Photo by E. Kay Trimberger)

THE CHALLENGE AND LURE
OF CREATIVITY

Art is the only way to run away without leaving home.[9]
— TWYLA THARP, quoted in Robert Greskovic,
"A Dance Master Does Dylan"

Rachel Rosenthal

REALIZING MY DREAM: TOHUBOHU!

The author created the life she wanted – as a theatrical artist

I will be 88 years old in November 2014 and have created the life I wanted. As a child I dreamed of becoming an artist who performed without a net, so to speak, and it took all my life to make it happen...I never liked rehearsals. I came alive in front of an audience. I did and said things that surprised even me. I think I was channeling, but in those days, didn't know the word. I studied visual arts, traveled as a political refugee all over the globe and alighted at the New York City High School of Music and Art, the great liberator. Over decades, I was torn between visual art and theater. I ended up as a theatrical artist, with the visual arts trailing not far behind. Although I participated in conventional theater, my dream was always the unplanned, unscripted, unrehearsed, unrepeatable magic of free improvisation. Years passed unnoticed by me because I lived in the moment – in the now – and still do. In the 1970s and 1980s I became a solo performer – doing original pieces that were written and rehearsed – but always with a sprinkle of improvisation woven through. And now I have plunged fearlessly into my impossible dream of guiding a company where pieces are created completely in the moment.

This art form – difficult and unique – demands a certain kind of person, patient, dedicated, willing to wait and watch for the blossoming moment, willing to accept the unknown and to let a fabulous piece disappear into the cosmos even as it is being performed. Such people are rare; they need to be prepared to be fully themselves while also becoming part of a collective heart and brain.

I stopped performing in 2000, but I didn't stop teaching and developing my dream of total improvisation. I call this form TOHUBOHU! – an ancient Hebrew term for chaos. My physical capabilities are somewhat diminished but I have all my marbles and I am surrounded by people who believe in TOHUBOHU!

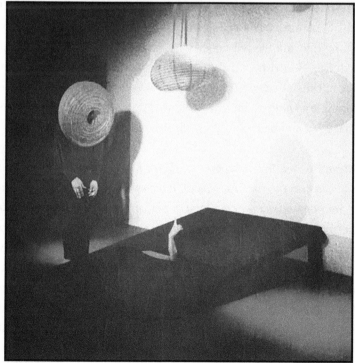

TOHUBOHU! 2014
(Photos by Kate Noonan)

We keep developing the form, the approach, the philosophy, and the performing in weekly workshops and monthly public performances. We have realized my dream, and still there are surprises, amazements, and disbelief. The capacity to create form, content, emotional material, and high style is unending. In spite of my health problems that have caused me pain, I can witness the results of our labors and gain unending inspiration.

There is no goal to be attained. No specificity to achieve.

What counts is making art. We create it out of nothing, arriving on the boards empty of intellectual causes and able to sustain close to two hours of beautiful and surprising work. There are no stars. Every performer acknowledges a change in daily life because of involvement in TOHUBOHU!

What happens on stage is a glittering echo of what life is like. Objects are imbued with magic. Lights, colors, shapes transform our material moment to moment – defining new horizons that constantly change one's trajectory. I watch from my chair and marvel. I tell myself, "You have seen a beautiful piece of art. You and the few people sitting here are the only ones who will ever see it." No one weeps. It's like life. Sometimes it flows continuously – sometimes it's interrupted; but it's always vibrant and real. My physical pains disappear. For a couple of hours I am free. My mind rarely wanders. I am focused on what I see and hear coming from the stage. I am happy.

Rachel Rosenthal, a winner of Obie, Rockefeller, Getty, NEA and CAA awards, among others, was an internationally recognized pioneer in the field of feminist and ecological performance art. Her revolutionary performance technique integrates text, movement, voice, choreography, improvisation, dramatic lighting and wildly imaginative sets into an unforgettable theatrical experience. Retiring from the stage in the year 2000, she continued teaching her signature brand of improvisational theater at her studio space and served as Artistic Director of The Rachel Rosenthal Company's TOHUBOHU! Extreme Theatre Ensemble. In 2000, the City of Los Angeles awarded her the title of Living Cultural Treasure. Rosenthal's work centered around the issue of humanity's place on the planet. She was an animal rights activist, a vegetarian, and companion to an outstanding theater dog, Fanny. Rachel Rosenthal passed away May 10, 2015. When asked in an interview what she would like her epitaph to read, she said, "She served the Earth, and she was fun." She submitted this narrative in 2014.

Rachel Rosenthal and Fanny, 2012
(Photo by Martin Cohen)

I change myself, I change the world.[10]
– GLORIA E. ANZALDÚA,
Borderlands/La Frontera

Elise Dirlam Ching

BEYOND THE CHRYSALIS

The author considers her legacy

* * *

How shocking
to shed your chrysalis
and cling there wet and helpless
until blood and time
wind and sun
lift open your imago wings

* * *

Conversations about dying were not common in our family or community when I was growing up. Yet with hospice now guiding end-of-life care and death cafes popping up all over, death talk is no longer taboo. After losing both parents in my forties, I realized I was the next generation to die, and I wanted to be more mindful along the continuum of living and dying.

Entering my sixties, I ask myself, What is my legacy? No children and grandchildren. No rambling estate. No grand invention or Einsteinian theory. It is the legacy of the moment each day asking, What brings my life meaning? and staying open to the shifting answers, even when they make me squirm. Loving the tough questions, being willing to fight with them, sit with them, share them, can be a gift for any age. Would my mother and her mother think so? What kind of a conversation might we have around the kitchen table now? Sometimes in my inner world I go there, and I imagine they are pleased.

My first date with my now-husband of 25 years was to Qigong (energy cultivation) class. Soon after, Kaleo, an artist, began teaching maskmaking and art-as-healing classes at John F. Kennedy University. I'd assist and we'd include Qigong to engage the body. I'd then guide students on journeys into subconscious realms, where they encountered the sacred wisdom of their souls, which would then emerge through painting, collage, or maskmaking. Once finished, students shared their stories of healing, discovery, and transformation.

In my fifties, grounded in my studies in English, transpersonal psychology, hypnotherapy, and Chinese medicine/Qigong, I began, with Kaleo, to put the journeys, processes, and stories from our years of teaching together into writing. Five books have emerged as a result. When we teach and write together, part of the challenge and the joy is bringing to the surface the important questions, knowing that, for each person and for different times in one's life, those will be different.

Sometimes sexy, sometimes brutal, sometimes confounding, sometimes delightful, writing is everything but easy. We just delivered our most recent book into our publisher's hands at North Atlantic Books. I feel limp and dizzy, like a new butterfly. Writing *The Creative Art of Living, Dying, and Renewal: Your Journey through Stories, Qigong Meditation, Journaling, and Art,* about the cycles of living and dying, within this life as we know it and beyond, has been a sweaty labor of love – mounting, pausing, mounting again, over the past several months. The result is an invitation to the reader to approach every phase and challenge of life, including its ending, with awareness.

LOVE AND WAR

Sliver moon rises before dawn
nibbled to a shred of her former self
not protesting the desecration–
no less beautiful the unseen

Hummingbirds dueling
in loops and dives
pause in the shadows
of an open flower
Stags with antlers locked
stagger down the hill
then exhausted in their closeness
slip apart and turn away

Sometimes
love and war
must sit together
and both be still.

6/1/14

Elise Dirlam Ching, RN, MA. Elise and her husband, Kaleo, coau-
thored several books, including The Creative Art of Living Dying &
Renewal *and* Chi and Creativity. *They have co-taught Qigong and art-*
as-healing classes for the past 23 years at John F. Kennedy University
and many institutions in the San Francisco Bay area and beyond. See
their gallery of poetry and art at www.kaleoching.com.

Elise Dirlam Ching and her husband, Kaleo Ching, at home, 2006
(Photo by Lyn Moreno)

Elise Dirlam Ching, 2008
(Photo by Kaleo Ching)

You can't sit around waiting for somebody else to say who you
are. You need to write it and paint it and do it.
That's the power of being an artist.[11]

– FAITH RINGGOLD, quoted in Alexxa Gotthardt,
    "The Enduring Power of Faith Ringgold's Art"

Jean Fineberg

FROM BLOWING HOT AIR
TO HITTING THINGS

Professional saxophonist, drummer…what's next?

Jean Fineberg, 2016
(Photo by Jane Higgins)

Ihave always been a musician. My mother, a professional dancer, started me on piano at age six. In fourth grade I took violin lessons, and in seventh I switched to flute. I played regularly in school orchestra, band and marching band. Each summer from ages 12 to 17, I went to Beaverbrook Music Camp in Pennsylvania. Most of the campers were very serious about music, and it wasn't unusual to see them skipping their swimming or horseback riding time to go off and practice in the woods (at least that's what they said they were doing!). I started out in camp as number 23 of 23 flutes, and by the last year, I was first chair.

I earned two bachelor's degrees and a master's in music education in liberal arts and sciences, science education, and educational psychology from Penn State. In graduate school, I assembled a drum set from pots and pans, endearing myself to my neighbors.

After college, I drove to San Francisco to be part of the hippie movement. The commune I joined had a drum kit, and I fooled around on it and carried my flute wherever I went.

Back in New York City, I became serious about the saxophone. I studied privately and joined the seminal women's original rock band Isis, with whom I toured and recorded three albums, which included my compositions and/or arrangements.

I frequented rehearsal bands and sought every opportunity to play. Isis went to New Orleans to record, and there I met my life partner-to-be, trumpeter Ellen Seeling. We became a tight horn section and formed the all-original jazz/funk horn group DEUCE, playing primarily my compositions. DEUCE toured nationally and recorded two albums. I also recorded and toured on saxophone with David Bowie, with Chic on "Freak Out," and with Sister Sledge on "We Are Family" and toured Europe with iconic trombonist Melba Liston's octet.

Ellen and I moved to California, where I teach saxophone and flute at the California Jazz Conservatory, in Berkeley, and play sax in several ensembles. I am the assistant director of the Montclair Women's Big Band, in which I play lead tenor sax.

At age 61, I decided to become a drummer. I took every drum class the Conservatory offered and studied privately. My garage drum studio delivers almost daily ambient thumping to our new neighbors.

After numerous auditions, I ended up in a Jimmy Buffett tribute band, which definitely kicked up my drumming several notches. I then joined a punk band, which really stretched my skills.

I assumed that I could be only a rock/funk drummer, because I didn't have enough years left to become a good jazz drummer, no less a traditional big band drummer. Then one of my sax students told me that the Albany, California, Jazz Band was looking for a drummer, and I now play drums with them and the Class Act Big Band.

One New Year's Eve, a producer asked me to provide a dance band, assuming that I would play sax. I called on my best professional musician friends, installed myself on drums, and The Party Monsters was born. I spend countless hours booking the band, and I'm thrilled that we have done seven to ten paying gigs a year at festivals, private parties and clubs.

It was strange for my musician colleagues to see me on drums instead of sax, but most of my income now comes from playing both instruments. I am having the time of my life; there is nothing more fun than driving a big band from the drum chair or rocking out with all the power that the drummer has.

Of course, I frequently need to haul a good deal of heavy equipment. I welcome the exercise and I love building my schlepping (as well as playing) muscles. I intend to keep gigging on drums until I'm about 90. Then I will reassess things. At that point, I may need to hire a roadie to help haul my drums to gigs.

Jean Fineberg (1946–2056) adopted a 12-year-old at age 60, got her most recent tattoo at age 67, and was married for the first time, to Ellen Seeling, at age 68. Her original big band charts are to be recorded by the Montclair Women's Big Band and published by her company, Bodybuilder Music, when she is 69.

Jean Fineberg, Sunnyvale, California, 2014

Judith Newton

THE DOOR IS ONLY A DOOR

Retired from academia, now a full-time writer…
but screenwriting?

Earlier today I read about a screenwriting conference to be held mid-August 2014 in Los Angeles. The conference is to include the usual workshops, speakers, and panels along with a "pitch slam" – a chaotic, noise-filled event at which a hundred or so screenwriters line up to describe their scripts to agents and producers. The screenwriter's two minute pitch is followed by three minutes of critique from the agent.

Were I to attend this conference, I'm fairly certain I would be the oldest person there. (I've seen pictures of these gatherings, and aspiring screenwriters, along with most agents and producers, appear to be pushing twenty-seven.) I can already imagine the awkwardness, the possible alienation, I might experience, and yet I'm strongly thinking about going and paying to do the pitch. (Imagine speed dating in which it's understood that all your "dates" are there for the express purpose of being critical.)

That I even think about participating in an event like this is the result of a policy I took up shortly after I retired – I'll call it the policy of the open door. I'd been an academic writing academic books for forty years, but in 2009, six months after I retired, I decided to write for myself. There were some long-simmering feelings and experiences I needed to come to terms with. I'd do so by putting them into words and I'd see what else, if anything, would develop.

That I'd already had a career was immensely useful to this project. When I took up writing memoirs, I didn't have to prove myself. I'd already done that in a prior life. I felt free to be a beginner, free to fail. I decided, however, that if any doors were to open for my writing, doors to a larger audience, for example, I'd step through them. And so I enrolled in writing classes, was eventually approached about contributing to a collective blog (by one of my classmates), developed my own blog, and eventually published a memoir, *Tasting Home,* in 2013. It went on to win some prizes.

Based on the demography of my memoir classes, I'd say that a lot of women my age are writing memoirs. We belong to a generation of women who've brought about enormous changes, and I think a lot of us want to make sense of what we've lived through. Many in this same generation worked outside the home in numbers greater than the U.S. had seen before. Working outside the home for most of your life can affect the way you organize your older age.

After forty years in academia, for example, I found the idea of retirement vaguely threatening. Yes, I was tired, but the idea of *not* working seemed deeply unsettling. I was used to the discipline and to the meaning my work had given my life (I was director of a women's studies program), and I was fond of the creativity it allowed me to express. I wasn't sure how I would center my life without some kind of work. And so I continued writing, which had been one of my favorite activities as an academic, although this time I had to learn how not to sound like one.

Stepping through open doors was not always a piece of cake. Writing a memoir was sometimes depressing, and it was a lot of work. Looking for doors to open, nonetheless, has become habitual. Last December, it occurred to me that my memoir could be a screenplay. I read five books on how to write a screenplay, wrote a screenplay based on my memoir, had it critiqued by a director (the husband of a friend), and took a screenwriting class.

Although I know Hollywood is inclined to action, adventure, and to anything written by men for other men, I am thinking of taking my female-centered story to this conference and shopping it around. I could fail big time, but if I ignore this open door, how will I feel? I have decided to walk through it, knowing that, to paraphrase Adrienne Rich, a door is only a door; it makes no promises.

Editor's Note: Judith attended the conference, a workshop leader critiqued and transformed her pitch. She delivered it at five tables, cried twice – a "no, no" at a pitch fest – and received requests for a synopsis from four tables; two women requested the entire screenplay. She awaits a response.

Judith Newton is Professor Emerita of Women and Gender Studies at UC Davis. Her memoir, Tasting Home, *organized by decade and by cookbooks that shaped the author's life, offers a journey through the cuisines, cultural spirit, and politics of the 1940s through the 2000s. It came out in 2013 with She Writes Press and has won ten independent press awards. It comes with recipes.*

Judith Newton, Berkeley, California, 2008

An artist paints, dances, draws, writes, designs, or acts at the expanding edge of consciousness. We press into the unknown rather than the known. This makes life lovely and lively.[12]

— JULIA CAMERON, quoted in Sara Douchette,
"25 quotes on Innovation and Creativity"

Petronila Tabudlo Blank

Bridging Cultures

*Disabled and retired, the author reached a
turning point in her life*

Petronila Tabudlo Blank, Memorial for a friend, Hawai'i, 2007

I was born in the Philippines in 1946. Two months later my family moved to a sugar plantation on Hawai'i. We were a hard-working, self-sustaining family. My parents taught us to work hard. We grew produce and raised livestock. After high school, I worked as an au pair and attended community college on Oahu, then worked for 10 years as a dental assistant.

After eight years of marriage, I found myself divorced and living in California. Then the real love of my life came into the picture and I remarried. We are still madly in love and happily married almost 40 years later.

My husband got me into the sales industry. The more I learned from him, the better I got at sales. I loved being my own boss, and eventually I hired my husband. I did this work for 20 years.

With health issues starting, I began to learn about alternative ways to heal myself, and I'm glad I did.

THE CHALLENGE & LURE OF CREATIVITY

This is also when I started to sense an inner urging that there was more to learn from nature, the universe, even from within me. I learned about self-help and empowerment and dabbled in stone power and crystals, aromatherapy and such.

In 2001 my husband and I cut short a business venture and moved to the island of Hawai'i after he injured his back and decided to retire.

Disabled at 58, I retired, and that inner urging started again. Wanting to know more about life, I attended a workshop on Hawaiian shamanism and learned about spirituality. This was a turning point in my life, a very empowering stage. Here is where I finally connected and realized that Hawai'i is more than just a place; it is home. The path has opened, and I'm on it.

This was an opportunity to learn about Hawai'i from the *kumus* (teachers) who share the knowledge and wisdom of the ancient ones. Fascinating. Like a child thirsting for information, I studied and practiced whatever resonated with me. Wanting to take care of my health, I learned *la'au lapa'au* (plant medicine), healing touch, Reiki, theta, lomilomi, even mediation. This journey opened my eyes and heart to life and how we are all connected to everything and everyone. We all are, after all, energy, vibration, frequency.

In 2005, at age 59, I traveled alone to Japan, although I did not speak or understand the language. There, I experienced a past life and saw that I was a doctor married to a Japanese general. We had two daughters and I had a sister. I've recently connected to my sister and my daughters. What an awesome feeling.

While there, I dreamt about an older man who told me to bring the knowledge and wisdom of the ancestors of the Philippines to the youth and children in Hawai'i and the world. The older man was my grandfather Leon Pira, whom I hadn't met. He is the reason I am doing what I'm doing now. My uncle confirmed that Pira, a shaman in the Philippines, was the man in my dreams when I exactly described him. After dreaming about him again, I went to the 1st Babaylan International Filipino Conference, held at Sonoma State University in 2010. When I returned home to Hawai'i, I had the first ever workshop on the Ancient Healing Arts of the Philippines. This same elder in my dreams said to go deeper, and through a computer search, I connected to Pi Villaraza who came to Hawai'i in 2011 to teach about self-sustainability and inner dance. I then started a nonprofit organization called Balitok Nga lma, the Golden Healing Hands.

The following year, I traveled to the Philippines again to learn more about self-sustainability and inner dance. There I learned how one can live on just coconuts, becoming more relaxed, letting everything flow, just being: having clarity, being more creative, being happy, being in the moment.

Now back in Hawai'i, I still love coconuts and got a few other people hooked on them as well.

At age 68, truly loving myself, I believe everything happens for a reason. A child at heart, feeling blissful, I wake up grateful for all that I am and what I have.

I will always continue to learn and expand my horizons, because there is so much out there to learn about. The cosmos: That's a story in itself.

I choose to BE. The Creator and the universe have orchestrated how to allow me to JUST BE.

Petronila Tabudlo Blank is a teacher and practitioner of lomilomi (Hawaiian massage), Reiki, Ha art (painting with one's breath), inner dance, healing plants and herbs and Bowl of Lights, learning not to take in negative energy. She is a practitioner of Kinetics Chain Release and Ito Thermie. She is also an ordained minister of the Church of Spiritual Humanism and has performed weddings, memorials and house blessings. You can view the Pi Villaraza workshop at https:// www.youtube.com/watch?v=AnvshzN09a8.

Petronila Tabudlo Blank at home, 2010

(W)hat was any art...but a mould (sic) in which to imprison
for a moment the shining elusive element which is
life itself – life hurrying past us and running away,
too strong to stop, too sweet to lose?[13]

— WILLA CATHER,
The Song of the Lark

Barbara Bosson

NOT QUITE A LIFE IN THE THEATRE
But still an actress

I vowed at an early age to become an actress. Later I wished I hadn't let someone so young make my career choice, but somehow it was indelibly imprinted, and it's the path I followed. During the 1950s, I had seen acting only on TV. Enthralled and not realizing how limited early television writing and acting were, I wanted to be in everyone's living room conveying some kind of message.

My parents were children of the Great Depression and seemed overwhelmed by the world they inherited. My father wanted to be a journalist but worked as a car salesman and a milkman. He never felt secure or fulfilled by his work. It taught me at least to try to do what made me happy.

My mom had good street cred: early American colonists, Revolutionary War vets, the person who brought the first anvil from Britain, Salem shipbuilders who travelled from Massachusetts to Ohio in covered wagons and settled it when it was the frontier.

Mom's dad was a John Henry (or steel man) at J.&L. Steel, with a managerial job. He moved his family to Belle Vernon, Pa., which sat in a little dark smoggy valley on the Monongahela River, where I was born. Interesting fact here: Mom's dad was anti-union, of course, and police had to walk my mother and her sibs to school because striking workers threw things at them during several bitter and violent work stoppages. This was before I was born, but it's ironic that I eventually served on the Board of the Screen Actors Guild and have always been an ardent union supporter.

When I went to New York at 18 to seek acting classes and work, my parents reluctantly let me go. Though trained to be a secretary, I naturally ended up working as a waitress for six years, until I got a job as a bunny at the newly opened New York Playboy Club. It took me three years to earn enough to audition and get into Carnegie Tech, now Carnegie Mellon, where I majored in drama. Work scholarships followed and as time went on, I became more sophisticated, started

Barbara Bosson and Dennis Dugan in NBC-TV's
"Richie Brockelman, Private Eye," 1978
(Press Photo)

learning about "The Theater" and traded my dream of television for one in which I would be a great lady of the theater. It's kind of ironic that for over 25 years, with running roles in six shows, I was a television actress, just as that very young Barbara had wished. My father died before I had any success; my mother saw me a little bit on TV and I know she was proud.

I got a job during the summer of 1967 in The Committee, a San Francisco improvisational theater company. The show brought me to L.A. and I worked at the Tiffany Theatre for two years. I re-met Steven Bochco, whom I had known at Carnegie Tech, and we were married in 1970.

My career really ended with my divorce in 1998. I had always worked pretty much alongside Steven, who wrote all my good roles. I had always felt close and involved in his shows, starting with "Hill Street Blues" and culminating with "Murder One." I received six Emmy nominations for these wonderful roles.

I suppose I could have tried to work for other people and I did, somewhat, but I was getting older and my health began to be a factor. I was diagnosed with fibromyalgia and lipedema, both amorphous but energy-sapping, painful conditions.

Fortunately, money wasn't an issue, so with little energy, a tendency to be pretty fragile in terms of depression, and no longer believing I could find any work better than what I had already done, I retired.

I missed acting a lot at first.

It took a few years but I found peace working with environmental issues. I co-formed a group called L.A. Bioneers with a friend and became educated in things such as global warming and natural sciences. I started a foundation to maximize the dollars I could give to environmental projects, began to have a fabulous garden and turned into a grandma junky.

I won't lie and say I don't still long for the kind of roles Maggie Smith and Judi Dench get, but they are the best of the best. Still a Life in the Theater would have been nice.

I'm happy; I don't mind growing old. I've let my hair grow grey because I've always hated beauty salons, and don't wear makeup because I think I'm prettier without it.

Barbara Bosson and her former husband, Steven Bochco, have two incredible and wonderful children, Jesse and Melissa. Barbara has one grandchild, Wesley Harrison Wrona, who is even more incredible and wonderful and wants to be a skateboard champion or pitch a no-hitter in Dodger Stadium.

Barbara Bosson, 2013

Judith Saldamando

"AYE, JUDY, YOU NEVER KNOW IN LIFE"

Lessons from an aunt

Tia Mary, 1981

"Aye, Judy, you never know in life," Tia Mary, my husband's Mexican-American aunt, so often declared over the decades of knowing her. Now in my early 70s reflecting back, I realize how frequently her words have proven to be true. When starting a family in my very late 30s and later when approaching middle age, I looked upon growing old with standard trepidation.

Tia's words, sounding so wise, were not helpful at that time. As I grew older, however, I began to experience how unknowns could also contain unpredictable possibilities.

During my years of raising children and caring for chronically ill Tia, I missed my earlier Bay Area activism in the second-wave feminist and civil rights movements and jobs with the farmworkers' and early environmental movements. Throughout those activist years, I also performed in experimental dance theatre. Such activities were a pushback to the cultural dictates of my youth. In the 1950s I had been discouraged from pursuing an interest in law or a career in art history or sculpture as being predominantly "male only" fields. As a result, my coming-of-young-adulthood period had at its core the "consciousness raising" of many "isms," including "ageism." "Aye, you never know…"

One of the unforeseen possibilities as an "older woman" was a job offer as an assistant teacher. This opportunity reflected a societal change in attitudes about age. Although I was older than even the mothers of the faculty members, I discovered that, in spite of continual energy challenges, my age would serve as an enriching resource as I could offer first-hand accounts of significantly recent historical events.

"Aye, you never know…"

My teaching community offered another unpredictable opportunity recalling my dance/theatre days. I received a grant to attend an improvisational theatre summer workshop in Santa Fe. As the "older woman" there, I needed to manage and overcome physical limitations from arthritis. Adding to those challenges, I had been tested for ovarian cancer just before leaving for Santa Fe and was fearful about learning the results. Once again, "you never know" came into play. The very nature of improvisation allowed me to incorporate the fear whenever it threatened to surface in my creative work. I returned home to good test results. In due time, however, job demands steadily aggravated my arthritis and signaled the time for retirement.

Then, just as I was reluctantly settling into retirement, another "aye, you never know" occurred. This time it's the recycling of experiences during the AIDS epidemic in San Francisco. A close friend, an anthropology professor, has begun writing a book about women who had created "families" for the isolated/forgotten men with HIV/AIDS. She has used our family, which included our beloved neighbor, for one model. Remembering and writing has repurposed those painful years as a testament to love, memory and an example of "you never know."

At this age now, my family remains my passion and love. With all of them living at very great distances, I nurture my mind with life-long learning classes (sadly unavailable to the previous generation) and my soul with drawing and writing. Sharing the aging process with close friends deepens this journey. I continue to wonder what the unknowns ahead might be with their unpredictable challenges but also their latent possibilities. Today, my own amazing ninety-nine year old mother would join Tia Mary in saying "You never know in life!" *Ojala* to all of you.

Judith Saldamando lives in San Francisco with her husband. With her master's in museum studies, she's been an educator at The Mexican Museum, SFMOMA and in SF schools. She travels to Brooklyn to visit her two children and to southern California to see her elderly but spirited mother.

Judith Saldamando, San Francisco, California, 2008

The journey in between what you once were, and who you are now becoming, is where the dance of life really takes place.[14]

— BARBARA DE ANGELIS,
How Did I Get Here?

Lori Goodman

NOT MY MOTHER

A life different from her mother's as the author ages

I feel I am and have been surrounded by extraordinary women, my mother, sisters, and daughters included: wise, fun, strong and principled. I certainly don't stand out in my crowd of amazing women. We are doctors, lawyers, politicians, artists, athletes, CEOs, newspaper publishers, teachers, psychologists, amazing cooks, community activists, musicians, you name it.

I was none of these as a younger woman. Well, I was co-owner of a fiber arts store, a long-time weaver, papermaker, runner, backpacker, and volunteer, but my primary role was wife and mother. A role which I relished (most of the time). I enjoyed being a mother and part-time artist, merchant, teacher. As I aged, my life deviated from that of my mother. At 50 I finished my master's degree in sculpture and, at the age of 60, I joined the Peace Corps.

In Belize I helped to strengthen girls' "at risk" groups that were producing crafts as a moneymaking business and skills-teaching opportunity. The girls' school where I taught papermaking continues with its program to this day. We received a grant for a paper beater, and the crafts director has become an excellent papermaker. I also procured a small kiosk in a tourist area where the girls, along with many Mayan women, worked and sold their crafts. It was still in business the last time I was in Belize.

This was my life-changing experience, certainly a departure from anything my mother would have done at this age. For some reason the Peace Corps gave me strength and confidence. I was totally without responsibility for anyone else and in charge of my own life and activities without anyone, including myself, saying "you can't do that." I realized that stuff can indeed happen – one can try anything. It may not work, but then again, it may, and anything that one thinks worthwhile is worth a try. I had no fear, and things of which I'm proud did get accomplished.

I returned home with a new determination to work full-time on my art.

**Lori Goodman and students preparing "At Bay,"
Humboldt State University, Arcata, California, 2008**

And I have. My medium is handmade paper. I seem to enjoy processes: I make the paper, construct armatures, and make the sculptures and installations. I fill rooms with paper and my own dwellings and artifacts.

I have not made it to MOMA, but I have had some minor success, many solo shows, some university shows; at 72 I'm not even close to being finished. Maybe I'll have my big show in Mexico because I recently started studying Spanish seriously. Regardless of public success, I am a maker and look forward to being one the rest of my life. I am still a serious mother, grandmother, walker, hiker, public arts advocate, traveler, reader and friend to many amazing older people.

Lori Goodman was born in a small town in Montana (according to Lori, that's the only kind there are). When she was ten, she and her family moved to Los Angeles, where she was exposed to the big city for the first time. She thinks, however, that the small town must have been in her. Lori loves big cities, travels to them often and has lived in a few but feels she belongs in the trees and on the beach in northern California (for now) where she can have the space to make art. Her website is www. loribgoodman.com.

**Lori Goodman,
Eureka, California, 2014**

Trina Nahm-Mijo
WHAT'S STILL ON MY BUCKET LIST?

More like her father than her mother

I am a third generation Korean-American who was born in the middle of the Pacific ocean in a place called Manoa Valley (filled with rainbows) on the island of Oahu in Hawai'i. My mom, Elizabeth Whang, was born in San Francisco and when she was six years old, she was sent on a big ship to Oahu with her younger sister, Mary, to be raised by their Aunt Ha Soo. Their own mother died of overwork, and their father didn't know what to do with girls. He kept their older brother, Paul, as is traditional in Asian culture.

Being raised by her aunt, a single woman who was educated and a social worker, was highly unusual in the 1920s and set a matriarchal tone which has resonated with my own feminist, Baby Boomer leanings. However, my own mother decided to become a stay-at-home mom once her children were born. I, on the other hand, followed my father's Asian and Protestant values of consistent, daily work-hard ethic and have never stopped working since I was 13 years old. Since both of my sons were born in the summer, I never took any leave from my position as a community college professor on the Big Island, either to give birth or to raise them. In 40 years of teaching, I have been absent 2 days.

I consider my childhood to be relatively carefree and stable, and I have enjoyed the beautiful environment that Hawai'i has to offer. In fact, in the 1970s, after I completed graduate school at UC Berkeley and as Oahu became more and more developed, I chose to make the island of Hawai'i my home because the island was still environmentally raw and lush. This is what called to me the most, that and being part of a thriving artistic community.

When I was asked to submit a piece for this project, what popped up for me was not what I'm doing now but what are the things I still want to do before I leave this physical body for ethers unknown. At this writing, I am a couple of months shy of 65, and really I feel 16, 35, 50, and 6 years old all at the same time on any given day. I don't think I've been "happier" in a "I've-experienced-alot-of-life-love-disappointment-and-surprise-sort-of-way" and really DO wake-up grateful everyday for how my life unfolded and meandered to where I am today. I feel I have touched the creative source, and this is what gives me the greatest joy.

I have a lot of academic achievements like delicious alphabet soup – B.A., M.Ed., M.P.H., PhD, even a recently acquired certificate in HLS (Hawaiian Lifestyles) at 64, but it is still dancing and creating dances that gives me ecstasy. I really tried to retire this passion a couple of years ago, but it kept biting at my heels and, truthfully, I feel the best is yet to come. Movement has been the great theme of my life – movement of the intellect, movement to other places, and especially movement of the spirit. So what's still left in my bucket list before I kick the bucket?

I still aspire to dance and create choreography for zero gravity. Who would be the audience? Aliens, of course! Preferably friendly ones. I'm contemplating learning to scuba dive this fall from a former student. I trust him. I'm contemplating parachuting out of a plane for my 70th Birthday. I love to dive deep – whether in air, water, or the unconscious mind.

Then there is the big dream of building a tree house on the property across the street from our house in Happy Homes. I am one step closer to achieving that dream in that I'm in the process of purchasing the property, which has a huge mango tree, lychee tree, and avocado tree on it. I want our house to be the first Pete Nelson Treehouse built in Hawai'i.

My husband and I saw travel and experiencing different environments and cultures with our children as the best education. It must have worked, because neither of our two sons wanted to get a higher education past community college. We "tripped the light fantastic," and vivid memories sustain us: climbing up the treacherous steep back of Chichen Itza Temple in Mexico with our 2- and 8-year-old sons because we missed the gentler "tourist approach" with the rope rail in the front; being the only "tourists" around when we visited Guatemala shortly after the Managua, Nicaragua earthquake and then narrowly missing getting washed away by a flash flood in Honduras; trekking 30 kilometers into the highlands of Thailand with a monk who wore flip flops on his feet.

Although I've traveled quite widely, there are still some places that are on my bucket list. I want to go to Tibet. I want to go to Aotearoa. I want to go to Peru.

I do want to write that book my dad kept encouraging me to write, but only if I can do it on a house boat on the Washington Sound. I also want to direct and produce a movie.

If I live a normal lifespan, I have only about 20 years to do all these things. I had better get busy.

Trina Nahm-Mijo has been teaching for 40 years at Hawai'i Community College in dance, psychology, expressive arts, and women's studies. She lives with her husband, Jerry, grown sons, Shayne and Renge, and three dogs and three cats on a 1.5-acre ohana (family) farm on the Big Island.

Trina Nahm-Mijo, Hawai'i, 2010

Ellen Seeling

ON BEING A WOMAN JAZZ TRUMPET PLAYER

A professional musician fights misogyny

Ellen Seeling, 2009

I am 65 and have been a trumpet player since I was about 12. Before that, in the 1950s, I did lots of things girls weren't supposed to do – shoot guns, hunt, fish, and play sports all the time. Luckily my parents never told their daughters, us girls, that the things we wanted to do were for boys, not for girls.

I started playing professionally with local big bands in the Milwaukee area when I was 16 and got totally hooked on making money playing the trumpet and playing jazz.

With a university degree in Jazz Studies, I moved to New York City in 1975 and began touring and recording with Laura Nyro, Chic, Sister Sledge, Luther Vandross, the all-woman band Isis, the Machito Orchestra, Ray Barretto, Latin Fever and others. With saxophonist Jean Fineberg, who is now my wife, I also founded and led one of the first jazz fusion bands fronted by women, DEUCE.

After 15 years in Hell's Kitchen, Jean and I were burned out on life in the big city and moved to the San Francisco Bay Area. We have been living in the East Bay near Berkeley for 25 years and love it! We founded the Montclair Women's Big Band. I also began teaching private trumpet lessons and am currently a jazz trumpet instructor at UC Berkeley. I love teaching the trumpet and have attracted many girls and women as students. This is unusual for any trumpet teacher, as the instrument is still very much identified with males, especially in jazz.

I have become radicalized after almost 50 years of playing trumpet professionally and experiencing a tremendous amount of gender discrimination along the way. Instrumental jazz musicians and trumpet players in general are very misogynistic. In recent years I have spent more and more time fighting this discrimination.

I'm sure my mom, who is 84 and really a feminist at heart, would never have taken on this issue in a public way. She cringes at what she calls "shrill feminists," but given who she is, I really don't understand her attitude. She just thinks it's unseemly to protest or complain about personal things, especially about the condition of women.

Because of my current actions, I'm very different from my mom's generation. Working with two law firms, I'm trying to convince or force Jazz at Lincoln Center to include women among the permanent members of its orchestra, which has not had a permanent woman member in its more than 26-year history. I've attempted to raise consciousness about how women jazz musicians are excluded at every level – in education, performance, recording, in the jazz press, among jazz award winners, everything. I also founded and co-direct with Jean the only summer jazz camp for girls with an all-woman pro faculty anywhere in the world.

My health is very good, although I confess to having less energy than when I was younger. I also have less drive when it comes to finding performance opportunities for my big band and for myself. So far, I can still play the trumpet at a pretty high level, but I'm starting to understand why many people consider the instrument physically demanding. I feel that I have a couple more projects to finish, and then I'm done. I want to do one more recording with my big band and finish my legal action against the Jazz at Lincoln Center Orchestra. Then I want to retire and do things that are quieter.

Right now the things I enjoy most are quiet days at home, especially if my wife is here with me. I've come to appreciate my garden and plan to learn to can and preserve food and essentially do some urban homesteading. I've recently begun to read again, as I'd been too busy for many years to do much but work. I like seeing my trumpet students progress, have fun, grow good at playing the instrument, and become assets to their school bands. It's very gratifying. I probably will continue to teach part-time for as long as I enjoy it and can get around pretty well on the horn.

I think I've been very lucky and have lived a very unusual life for a girl from the Midwest. I'm very thankful that I will be able to stop working soon and have some fun.

Ellen Seeling was born in 1950 in Waukesha, Wisconsin, the oldest of six children. In 1969 she enrolled at Indiana University and in 1975 was the first woman to earn a degree in Jazz Studies there. Jean Fineberg and Ellen were married in 2014 after 39 years together.

Jean Fineberg and Ellen Seeling, New York City, New York, 1986

Patricia A. Murphy

TIME'S MESSAGES TO MY BODY

Two paintings inform the author's younger and older selves

As I age I find that I want to explore movement, stillness, and the between of these two states. I feel time's roar rushing me on and, at the same time, the quiet stillness of the infinite. This gift of time is resident in my body, my body which moves, experiences stillness when I practice tai chi or yoga or meditation, and that place between, which is awareness, soul force, me.

Two paintings in my home hang beside an archway which leads to a hall. The painting on the left is a torso portrait of me painted by Clarity Haynes at the 2005 Michigan Womyn's Music Festival. My torso is without breasts but with faint pink scars, lines softly tracing the nearly flat swell of my chest wall where my breasts used to be. Because of my immersion in disability studies, I did not regard the breast cancer as a tragedy. Prior to the surgery, I had a party for my breasts. I figured that I had had them for 52 years and they deserved some sort of celebration or, as I thought of it: Thanks and Goodbye. Fifteen women came to my house and we had food and wine and made a plaster cast of my breasts.

The painting on the right side of the arch is by the noted neo-renaissance portrait painter Leslie Adams. She has painted bishops, governors, and other dignitaries, but this piece is from her Eve Series. The painting was given to me by the Advisory Board of the Catharine S. Eberly Center for Women as my retirement gift. This Eve is a young woman and the Board members said, "It's you, Pat. Look at her nose. Your nose is like that." She is in profile and she has long blonde hair and she holds a nearly translucent sphere in her cupped hands. A brown robe or coat slips off her left shoulder, and this too is reflective of me because in my twenties, I spent a great deal of time taking off my clothing. Behind her is a blackboard with the uppercase alphabet on a chalk line from left to right, and beneath that the alphabet repeated in lowercase. The decimal system is also listed: 1, 2, 3, 4, 5, 6, 7, 8,

9, 0. Red outlines apples, hearts, flowers, and the grade C. A bubble in chalk white rises from the sphere. What is it? A crystal ball? A globe? The Eve Series reveals Eve as a scientist. That is, she conducts empirical research when she bites into the mythic apple from the Tree of Knowledge. I think of this Eve as the "Seeker." She is looking for knowledge in language, mathematics, and in the unknown or dimly perceived. She is me as a young woman, wild with long blonde hair wanting to know everyone and everything. Hungry.

Memory passes back and forth between these two images and I know that I am both young and old and something more now. The third image is me as I move through the arch to and from the minutiae of my present life. Perhaps I am exploring the between now, that essence which informs memory, body, self, stillness and movement.

Patricia A. Murphy lives outside of Santa Fe in the country surrounded by mountains, junipers, wild flowers, birds, rabbits, and coyotes. She is semi-retired, still teaching for the University of Toledo and Santa Fe Community College. Her teaching is focused on feminist disability issues, and she is the author of two novels, three nonfiction books, and several essays. She is currently working on a climate change novel.

Patricia A. Murphy at home, 2014

OVERCOMING ADVERSITY

You may not control all the events that happen to you,
but you can decide not to be reduced by them.[15]

       — MAYA ANGELOU,
       Letter to My Daughter

Victoria Emmons

THE LIST

Achieving life's goals while grieving a spouse's death

I moved to Northern California in 1985 from Florida. Jack followed me and we were married two years later. After a decade in Fremont, we moved across the bay to Los Altos to live closer to my job. As part of the move, the corkboard in my home office had to be dismantled. And there underneath the layers of life was my list.

The list had hung on the corkboard wall for years. It outlined my biggest dreams. If I wrote down the goals, they might come true. Over time, the list got covered up with magazine articles, postcard reminders and my daughter's artwork.

From long-term to more practical short-term goals, the list included those achievements that I wanted most. I knew they would be tough to do and there would be obstacles to overcome. I tucked the list among my other papers as part of the move and posted it on a new corkboard. I never gave up on those goals:

1. Earn a masters degree.
2. Buy a house.
3. Start saving for retirement.
4. Be elected president of my Rotary Club.
5. Send Kate to private school.
6. Save enough money for Kate's college.
7. Become a certified fundraising Executive.
8. Lose weight.
9. Become a CEO.
10. Publish a novel.

In 1999, Jack moved his business to Pleasanton, necessitating another relocation. This time, I would be the one to commute. While unpacking boxes at the new house, I discovered the list. By then, numbers 1 through 5 had been accomplished. I was still working on the rest. A decade later, I had achieved numbers 6 through 9. The elusive number 10 still remained on the list. I had been writing for years.

I knew I could achieve that last goal, even at age 59. Women writers my senior had won acclaim for their work. Surely I could publish a novel.

I started writing more. My characters began to live inside my head. I wrote dialog while commuting. I noted character traits in my diary. The lives of people in my novel were all-consuming and I began to ignore my real life. Then an obstacle appeared that caused my mind to go blank. My husband was dying.

For the next year, I focused on caregiving and planning a wedding. Our daughter was getting married that next summer. While my husband suffered chemotherapy, the most I could write was invitation lists. I was in denial.

Jack died a week before the wedding. I was in shock. How could he die? I staged a funeral and a wedding all in the same week.

A few days after the out-of-town guests had departed, my new life unveiled itself. The loneliness and empty feeling were overwhelming but expected. What I did not expect was my desire to write poetry. The words tumbled out of my head ... poems landing by the mouthful. Each line expressed my sorrow, my pain and my loss. My colleagues encouraged me to submit my work to an upcoming anthology.

At last, I was close to achieving number 10 on my list. It wasn't the novel I had planned but instead a series of sad poems that allowed me to breathe, allowed me to cry and allowed me to be me.

My mother wrote poetry. She never had anything published, but her family benefited from her delightful rhyming words over the years. I know she would be proud of me for having my poems now published in three anthologies. I have written enough for my own book of poetry and plan to publish it within the year. I haven't forgotten about the novel. It will happen someday. No matter what obstacles, I will publish that novel. I will complete number 10 on my list. And then I will start a new list.

SOLE SURVIVOR

I am the sole guest
At my dinner table
No one to please
Save my own palate

The hour is late
As work takes over
On this holiday week
With no one to share

A Roomful of Blues
Plays Solid Jam
    Awakening my soul
    Soul of another kind

    I scour cookbooks
    For fresh recipes
    Savor Gouda and gherkins
    With a vodka chase

    My kitchen dance begins
    10 o'clock piano jazz
    And smooth lyrics
    To hide my fears

    Let me love you, baby
    He repeats throughout
    A tune that will fade
    As love fades, too, after awhile

    Butter sizzles in the pan
    Hot pools of taste
    Wait for the main dish
    Washed and patted dry

Flour encases the fillets
Protects them from harm
Wish it were so easy
To protect me, too

Wrapped in flour
Browned and moist
Seasoned well over time
Sole Meunière survives

Victoria Emmons writes a column for Life on Foothill Road *magazine and publishes poetry and essays for the blog* La Vue de rue Sleidan *found at www.ruesleidan.wordpress.com. Her poetry appears in* Word Movers *and other anthologies. She is a mother and grandmother and has recently resigned as the CEO of a hospice.*

Victoria Emmons at home, 2013

Carolyn H. WarmSun

STARTING OVER ... AGAIN

Reinventing artistic pursuits as one ages
and develops infirmities

Parents young during the Great Depression, uneducated, poor and wanting their children to fare better, along with a small southern Indiana town with little to offer, set the stage for me to go to college and enter a profession that offered security. Mental health morphed into organization development consulting, from which I retired seven years ago.

In Hawai'i, while managing a women's mental health clinic, I took hula and danced. It was a great way to learn some of the culture. When I moved back to the mainland, I could not find hula close enough to me, so took up beginning ballet for adults. After three years, a foot injury stopped my dancing, and for several years I walked in great pain.

I started stone carving about a dozen years before retirement and loved it. I had been looking for woodcarving, having meant to pick up on that one experience in my only semester of art in high school, but stone was what I found. My wrists rebelled, but an acupuncturist healer kept me going until we moved from southern California to the San Francisco Bay Area and the painful tendonitis would no longer allow me to continue. I panicked. Retirement was coming in two years and I had worked all my life. I knew it would not be a happy thing for me to slam into retirement – I needed to find something meaningful that I loved.

I began once-a-week evening classes in painting at the local high school. I continued until I retired and then took classes at the local community college. It was OK, but I missed that "in flow" I had gotten carving alabaster sculpture – that sense of co-creating with the stone. A little more than two years after I retired, I was in my favorite used bookstore and pulled out a copy of Maxine Masterfield's *Painting the Spirit of Nature,* and my life changed. I went to Florida to spend four days with her. She showed me how painting can express the equivalent of one's experience of nature – not just replicate what one sees in nature. I came home transformed.

In a short period of time, I moved from painting by direction from whatever photograph a teacher handed me, to painting on my own from my own photographs, to painting the abstract essence of whatever comes out of my consciousness to my hands to the brush to the canvas.

My work is abstract. When I am finished, or nearly finished, I often see something that makes me think of the natural world, but not always.

Painting is a sacred practice for me, and my Studio is Church. My paintings are pieces

Carolyn H. WarmSun at home, 2014

of me. I am never happier than when the paint and I are creating something together, and I am using all my senses, problem solving as I go, fully and completely engaged. After this short amount of time, my hard work is paying off in awards and acceptances to prestigious shows.

Now, peripheral neuropathy has progressed to the point where I am often in pain. I am having to learn to listen to my feet, sit on a stool rather than stand, stop for a while. But injuries and pain have not stopped my pursuit of an arts practice in the past, and I vow to paint in whatever way I am able for as long as I am able. It is life.

Carolyn H. WarmSun was born July 9, 1942 in Vincennes, Indiana. She received a bachelor's degree from Southern Illinois University and a master's in social work from the University of Illinois, Campaign-Urbana. She worked in the mental health field for years, including the setting up of an independent program in women's mental health services for the State of Hawai'i. She retired in 2007 and lives with her husband, Larry Cooke, in Oakland, California. Her website is www.warmsunart.com.

Shura Saul

AT 74 – FINDING MY WAY IN MY OLDER YEARS

A new and full life after a spouse's death

I have just celebrated my 94th birthday. I don't know at what age a woman becomes a "little old lady," but I began to fit this description at 74, after my husband died unexpectedly.

Ours was a 62-year relationship and a 54-year marriage. Sidney Saul and I, one month apart in age, were friends from the time we were 12. Our families were summertime neighbors in Goldens Bridge Cooperative Colony, so I married the boy next door. We had a true love affair. We were a mutual support system and enjoyed parenting our three children. I began professional life as a kindergarten teacher. He graduated from City College of New York, was overseas in World War II, and became a social worker. We were involved in numerous left-wing social activities.

In the late 1950s, Sidney and I shifted our focus to the needs of older people. We became gerontologists during our forties, earned doctorates in our sixties, and worked together professionally whenever we could. In 1981, I organized the Bronx North Manhattan Coalition for the Elderly and Long-Term Care and, until 2001, when the organization ended, I wrote and published its newsletters, detailing its activities, which dealt with the seminal issues in gerontology.

After Sidney and I "retired," we worked in the Scottish mental health system for ten summers and volunteered in Israel.

We became grandparents. Always, we were together. These were our best times.

When he died, I didn't know how I could live or whether I wanted to. My children helped me find my way, and that's how this story begins.

Initially, along with grandmotherhood, I continued our prison work. Starting in 1992, Sidney and I had taught gerontology courses in a Mercy College program at New York's only high-security facility for women, Bedford Hills. In 1994, the federal government revoked scholarship aid to prison educational programs. I immediately helped organize a community group to restore college to the prison. With the warden's support, I also organized volunteer classes to maintain the program's continuity while we sought another college to provide a full program. By 2001-02, Marymount College started a program.

I had always been a writer, so I worked through much of my grief by writing poetry. I had always written and shared verses but never attempted to publish. My first effort was a booklet of poems titled *My Very Shadow Narrowed,* which I self-published in 1997. Psychotherapists, hospice workers, and friends in many parts of the world have used the booklet to work with grieving individuals.

My daughter and I shared our poetry, which we had never done before, and we self-published *Harmonies.* We added songs written by my daughter, choreographed dances, used family photographs to dramatize the book, and performed it with family and friends. Translated into Italian, it was performed at a cultural exchange program in Italy and U.S. venues.

In 1995, I began to study Italian and travel to Italy. My Italian teacher translated my poems for a self-published bilingual book, *La Bella Italia,* illustrated with photos from our trips. I also wrote and self-published a booklet of poems, *The View After Eighty.*

In 2001, my granddaughter was admitted to a performing arts high school in New York City and had to move there. I moved with her to a one-bedroom apartment and, three years later, her younger brother followed. While there, I began to mentor formerly incarcerated women who were continuing their studies and conducted a weekly in-service program for a nursing home. I was well into my eighties.

In 2006, I contracted lymphoma. After I recovered, my daughter and I co-wrote and published *Mother Daughter Duets: A Story-and-Workbook for Adult Daughters and Older Mothers.* To market it, we developed and conducted workshops for schools and community agencies.

Mercy College then suggested that I teach online courses in gerontology which I continue to do.

In 2010, when I turned 90, I wrote and published *From His Hands.* The book presents my husband's wood and ivory sculptures and describes his work and our life together. I also worked with my grandson, who wrote and directed a film about my life, work, and activism.

In 2013, I endured a second bout of cancer. Thanks to good medical treatment and superb care monitored by my daughter, I am in remission.

I don't get around easily any more. I use a cane and a walker, and I don't drive. But I consider myself a lucky "little old lady" to have supportive, loving adult children, delicious grandchildren and opportunities for continuity of work and interests.

Shura Saul is engaged in several projects that she fully expects to complete. These include writing and developing dramatic productions with the Pawling Shakespeare Club, teaching online, and developing children's stories that she wrote years ago. She and her Italian friend hope to publish the stories as bilingual books for young children.

Shura Saul, 2014

Sometimes good comes through adversity. I would not be who I am today had it not been for the internment, and I like who I am.[16]

– Ruth Asawa,
"Interview 1994"

Mary Kolada Scott

A GOOD EYE FOR ART

The author, a painter, deals with a vision crisis

At age five, I knew I wanted to be an artist, but it took me five decades to realize that dream. And I was lucky to have that chance.

My maternal grandmother had been a "Sunday painter." I admired her pastels and oils and wanted to be like her. Grandma, who had survived the Depression, discouraged me.

"Art doesn't pay," she'd say. "Be a nurse or teacher instead." I did neither.

When I was in junior high school, the art class was full, so I took creative writing instead. After the teacher got my first poem published, I was hooked. I switched my attention from visual arts to language arts and majored in journalism and creative writing in high school and college. I became a starving writer instead of a starving artist.

My grandmother's daughter – my mother – majored in journalism at university. She met my father, a typesetter, at a newspaper where they both worked. After they married, Mom wrote book reviews for a Catholic magazine and edited the parish newsletter. As my writing developed, my mother told me that she was proud of my accomplishments and awards and lived her dream through me. Still, Mom insisted I take typing because I could fall back on secretarial skills if writing didn't pay the bills.

After I married, I wrote freelance articles and published my poems. I dabbled in painting and crafts while raising a family, but I didn't take art classes until after menopause and an empty nest allowed me to focus on myself. With more time and discretionary income, I took my first watercolor class and started selling my work at local shows. I turned the guest room into a home studio and joined an art association. I continued to take classes and workshops in watercolor, printmaking and acrylic painting. I had my first solo show the year my first grandchild was born.

Mary Kolada Scott and her painting, "Winter Solstice," the first she painted after her eye surgeries, 2014

As I was growing as an artist, I faced a vision crisis. A routine eye exam to renew my reading glasses prescription revealed that I had advanced glaucoma. Undetected, the disease had already robbed me of considerable peripheral vision that couldn't be restored. I was referred to a local ophthalmologist who is an expert in glaucoma treatment.

When my condition didn't respond to medications and laser surgeries, I underwent a trabeculectomy on the more damaged eye in which a surgical drain was installed. Recovery was long and miserable, but the surgery was successful in keeping my pressure low.

Earlier this year, however, the doctor decided I needed the trab in the better eye to maintain the pressure and reduce the risk of more damage. In February, just after my 62nd birthday, I underwent surgery. I've also had two cataract surgeries.

Now as I paint, I am aware the time may come when I have to surrender to limited vision or blindness. I'm grateful that I didn't wait any longer to pursue my dream.

I continue to express myself through writing and art – when I write I find myself, when I paint I lose myself – and honor both my grandmother and mother. I look ahead to more advances in glaucoma treatment. Whatever my limitations are, I already have lived beyond the boundaries of my mother's and grandmother's narrow worlds.

And when I receive payment for my artwork, I remember what my grandmother said – art doesn't pay. For me, it does. When people tell me that seeing my work makes them happy, that's the ultimate payoff.

Mary Kolada Scott is a writer and artist whose poetry, articles, stories, photos and paintings have appeared in numerous newspapers, literary journals, galleries and poetry collections, including Her Mark, *a poetry and art date book produced by Woman Made Gallery in Chicago,* Calyx: a Journal of Art and Literature by Women, When Last on the Mountain: The View from Writers over 50, *and* The Disenfranchised: Stories of Life and Grief when an Ex-Spouse Dies. *Mary and her husband Don, a photographer, writer and editor, live in Ventura, California. Her website is marykoladascott.com.*

What is important is not the lucky break, the stopping of the train – that's only part of it. Life is full of trains that stop. What counts is what we are doing with our lives when there is no opportunity and not a train in sight.[17]

– Phyllis Whitney,
Guide to Fiction Writing

Mary Felstiner

Unforeseen

Poetry prompts creativity and resistance

Because a generation of daring young women brought about a feminist surge in the 1960s and '70s, reshaped the home and pushed into jobs never allowed before – because that generation of ours is growing old now, we're likely to gear up, all over again, for unforeseen lives. Some of us keep working for pay, needing to or choosing to. Some earn the privilege of retiring with pensions, assets, skills – another new stroke in history – while an unheralded number gets pressed back to old paths of family caregiving. And among all these maturing women, no one yet knows how many are still taking chancy swerves – only that our generation still goes unprecedented.

For myself, after three decades of teaching history in fluorescent-zapped classrooms at San Francisco State University, I retired to an unforeseen five years teaching new courses at Stanford, jumping into subjects as if just starting out. The last course I launched, Creative Resistance, carried its questions past my teaching years: Why have so many people turned to the arts, in private or secret, to thwart the aims of tyranny? And why, with survival at risk, would they perfect creative forms? Take Anne Frank, who two years after starting her diary rewrote it all into a work of art.

These questions reappeared in time for some creative resisting of my own – some efforts to thwart the aims of aging (with features in myself like rheumatoid arthritis and recurrent pneumonia). Models from the past made me wonder what would happen if I stopped prying into archives, hammering home conclusions – and started reaching for open-ended fictions. What might come of grasping the arts?

One answer – that grasping takes a lot of time – arrived pretty late. My first (sole) novel, concerning lust, murder, and plywood, needed seven years to stir and finish, before it flap-jacked off a laptop and onto a bottom shelf. After that I turned to another challenge, one that involved shutting up for a change. To create poems, for the first time, meant learning to suggest as much as possible with as little explanation, handing off to others, if they liked, all afterthought. True, I'm unqualified for this craft, and yet I'm struck how many applicable skills – sharing out interpretation, amassing ideas in supportive groups – I'd already learned from feminist classrooms.

It seems puzzling why someone in her 70s would use scarce runoffs of time to send bits of font along – by way of images, tempos, rhymes, all unseen, below the waterline. The reason may be that poems prompt a mind to get creative and at the same time resistant (say, inventing insoluble homework in "Problem Set" below). Or the reason may be that women my age become awestruck by simple intricate things, then search out simple intricate ways to relay them.

So, what keeps turning up, along the routes and ruts of aging? Unforeseen forms, and any of these might let loose – among harder surprises – explosive joy.

PROBLEM SET

Problem:
If your rheumatic hands splay like flippers,
how do you keep writing of other times,
since your passion – it's history
now, a thing of the past?

> *Solution. Just give up*
> *what's no longer yours.*

Problem:
Give up? Give up writing, say, about wars?

> *Solution. Wars are for not*
> *learning from. Go learn what*
> *you'll use, say, speech-recognition.*

Problem:
Speech-software fools with your diction.
You tell students, "Email me your section
preferences now" and your software sends:
"Email me your sexual preferences. Now!"

Solution. Sharp eyes on that screen.
Learn to stare.

Problem:

At a backlit square? And when your eyes
go rheumatic, dry as glass, seared by glare?

Solution. Stick to the shadows.
Only speak there.

Problem:

And when you can't speak longer even
there? When a used-up voice turns spare?

Solution. Ditch prose. Switch forms.
Tight lines. Less said.

Problem:

Less said – until unsaid words run
streaming down your nightgown
sleeves, out your fingernails, all gone
undone. Tight lines? None.

Solution. – Anyone?

Mary Felstiner taught
women's histories and his-
tories of genocide and pub-
lished a biography, To Paint
Her Life: Charlotte Salomon
in the Nazi Era *(1994), and*
a memoir/history, Out of
Joint: A Private and Public
Story of Arthritis *(2005).*
Recently she's turned, as a
novice, to writing fiction and
poetry.

Mary Felstiner at play, 2011

I NEVER THOUGHT I'D DO THIS

*The unexpectedness of life, waiting round every corner,
catches even wise women unawares.
To avoid corners altogether is, after all,
to refuse to live.*[18]

— FREYA STARK,
The Journey's Echo

Christie Batterman-Jordan

MY LIFE AS AN
AGING MERMAID SEX GODDESS

In the Caribbean, dressed in a monofin

Christie Batterman-Jordan, Big Sur, California, 2013

I am perched on the edge of the sailboat, about to glide my legs into the clear Caribbean water. It's tricky, though. My legs are encased in a silver mermaid tail. Below my feet, a wide, solid fin spreads gracefully, but it's heavy and difficult to move. My tail fin needs to cut through the surface, at just the right angle – otherwise, I'll belly-flop, ruining the scene.

At the age of 65, I am being filmed as a mermaid sex goddess.

Most professional mermaids, I have learned, are free-divers, able to hold their breath up to four minutes, supported by an off-camera crew with air supplies. But I am alone on a sailboat with my new, brilliant European boyfriend – he with the surprising and unexpected mermaid fascination – planning to film a thirty-minute mermaid story full of pirouettes and flirtations amid the coral reefs. I am wearing a scuba tank with sixty minutes of breathable air.

Do I feel sexy? A bit, but being under the water has always made me feel uneasy. My parents were New Yorkers, indoor intellectuals, and my father never learned how to swim. My mother loved being with friends on a beach, but I never once saw her put a toe in the water.

I might have stayed on the beach, too, if I hadn't given birth to two sons in my early forties. By the time they were teenagers, only adventure sports like scuba diving kept them enthusiastic about family vacations. We took to diving like a family of fishes, working our way through the levels of certification during enjoyable weeks traveling the world. We swam through underground caverns in Yucatan, around icebergs in Alaska, with manta rays, turtles, sea horses and bioluminescent jellyfish, thrilled to be exploring the oceans.

So when my new boyfriend suggested diving in the British Virgin Islands as a mermaid, I was excited. We commissioned a custom mermaid wetsuit with a special monofin to hold my feet in the tail. Then he dropped the challenge bomb: "Can you dive without a buoyancy compensator?" That's the vest recreational divers wear which works just like a fish's swim bladder – by adjusting its air content, you can stay comfortable and relaxed at any depth, but wearing a bulky vest would cover my breasts and destroy his mermaid illusion. Without my trusted diving vest, it would be up to my swimming skills alone to keep me positioned underwater for the camera.

And now here I am in the Caribbean, on a sailboat anchored in a shallow cove, palm trees gently waving in the tropical breeze. I take a lingering, last look at the sky and slip the silver tail into the water...and am instantly disoriented by the experience of trying to swim with my legs firmly held in place. I am sinking fast to the sandy bottom twenty-five feet below. "So far, nothing sexy at all about this experience!" I think as the air bubbles flow upward while I lie like a giant silver sardine, flopping on the ocean floor. In the meantime, my lover, who had been filming my entry, has joined me on the bottom, great concern showing in his eyes. And well-justified that concern is, since I had left all my wits at the surface. Finally, after a long interval of measured breathing and feeling calm, I lift my shoulders and kick firmly off the bottom.

Oh, what a ride! As I remember how to dolphin kick with my legs, my tail moves so swiftly that the coral sails by. I swim up or down gracefully, starting a sensual rocking motion by pulling my shoulders back and urging my waist forward. My hips follow in one long wave.

My tail echoes the rhythmic rocking of my hips. It propels me through the water. Fish swim by, seeming to welcome me as one of their own.

Sunbeams sparkle around me and I lift my head to see light dancing on the surface above. Gently kicking and bending backward, I make a perfect circle somersault, effortless and weightless, gliding with one smooth motion. Reaching my arms forward and legs back, I stretch out the full length of my tail and ride happily in the warm water toward a soft, sandy clearing in the coral reef.

Breathe. Settling into the sand, I am framed by sea fans and coral. Angel fish and a multitude of colorful tropical fish glide nearby like jewels in the water. My lover's eyes are smiling behind his video camera, about twenty feet away. He swims in ever-closer circles, his lens holding the mermaid in tight, loving focus.

I run my hands across my breasts then blow a kiss to him and his camera. © 2014

Christie Batterman-Jordan is an art historian and glass artist who founded a company that became one of the largest international suppliers of decorative glass. She balances her love for the arts with a passion for nature and tries to spend as much time outdoors as possible, hiking, gardening, birding and scuba diving. Mermaid videos can be seen on YouTube. Search for: UW videographer. Otter Bay Custom Wetsuits, Monterey, California made the mermaid wetsuit.

We all yearn for mastery. But mastery is always limited. Sooner or later we will come to the edge of all that we can control and find life, waiting there for us.[19]

— RACHEL NAOMI REMEN,
My Grandfather's Blessings

Anita Goldstein

HORIZONTAL STRIPES

It's all Improv

Horizontal stripes
Make you look fat;

Don't be too smart
Men don't like that

Don't be too loud;
Just make us proud

Words to live by? Not anymore.

And it's not ALL about horizontal stripes. I was expected to be intelligent and succeed (I was, I am and I did); the message, growing up in the '40s, was that even if I created something of my own, on my own, it would be of secondary importance to being married.

I did marry, in the 1950s, and my life followed a predictable course. I had a loving husband, wonderful kids, and a "good" marriage. All that ended when I decided not to cook anymore. Really! I'd made everything I knew how to cook many times over. And I began to resent not getting any acknowledgement or help.

I'd also tried everything I knew to make my marriage a partnership – that didn't work either. Whatever common language we might have started with turned into angry gibberish.

By then, women had been having "click" moments for a long time. I didn't hear them. I didn't need a hearing aid; I needed to hear myself.

My journey started at 50 when I attended sensory awareness classes at the New School for Social Research in New York. There I discovered I didn't only *have* a body; I *was* that body. I began to inhabit it and experience it. One day, as I drove home from the city to Larchmont on the very bumpy West Side Highway, I had an orgasm – my first one all my own.

It seems that the deeper I explore my life, the more I flourish. That awareness led to greater honesty in my relationships with my partner, children and friends. The deepening is not without some pain and confusion; but more often it fills me with a deep sense of accomplishment and ever-increasing access to my creativity.

I once asked my therapist, "Why am I still doing this? I'm 80 years old! Why does it matter anymore?"

She said, "It matters because it's your life." I can't argue with that.

My mother once asked why I would tell my "secrets" to a "stranger." Beyond the obvious response – that I don't want secrets and my therapist is no longer a stranger – I told her that being in therapy is, for me, like seeing a beautiful piece of sculpture. I look at one side, and it's beautiful and satisfying; then someone takes my hand and walks me all around it, and I am able to see the piece of art – my life – in all aspects of its beauty and imperfections. The wholeness and complexity are appealing to me. All is revealed.

Building community has always been a passion of mine. During my marriage we moved a lot, and we all needed to feel at home, so I just naturally connected with other families and gravitated toward involvement with community organizations. My mother was mistrustful of other women and tried to warn me about those connections. But I felt that for my family to be at "home" – wherever that was – we needed to be a presence in our community. I've been teased that I can create community in the locker room of the pool.

I started doing improv when I was 75. Doing Improv is the true "horizontal stripe" of my life. It's showing off, being "loud" and inviting attention. Improv is a form of theater where what is performed is created at the moment it is performed. There is no script, and no safety net other than the support of the other performers on the stage. I study Improv at Stagebridge in Oakland, California, and BATS in San Francisco. The Stagebridge improv troupe I perform with is called The Antic Witties.

I *AM* an old woman, showing off. When I'm in the flow of doing improv in class or in front of an audience, I have no awareness of the audience, and I don't feel old. I DO have exhilarating moments of high-wire panic. I've always yearned to be seen and heard. It's not possible to demur, to BE demure – AND to be seen.

In improv we learn a gesture of surrender for when we've goofed: We raise our arms, smile, and shout: "Ta Da" to acknowledge a flub. And then we carry on. It's a terrific life lesson for me.

As performers, and as human beings, we don't know what we're actually going to do; our "audience" certainly doesn't know – so whatever the risk, it's all worth it; it's all improvised. Ta Da!

Anita Goldstein was born in Buffalo, New York in 1932. Middle child, only girl, she received a master's in education when she was 50. Anita became a teacher as a way to be able to support herself. She taught reading for a short time, then moved to California. Proposition 13 meant no jobs for reading teachers. Anita worked in L.A. at the Pritikin Longevity Center; then in public relations at the University of Southern California for 11 years. She moved to El Cerrito, California, when her grandson was born in 1995. Anita and her partner, Paul, have been together since 1985.

Anita Goldstein at home, 2014
(Photo by Nancy Rubin)

B. Lynn Goodwin

TWO ROADSTERS ON THE SUPERHIGHWAY

Love, not cars, late(r) in life

B. Lynn Goodwin and her husband, Richard Brown, Danville, California, 2011

" 1944 classic roadster with many miles left!
    Motor humms, transmission smooth and all the gears work!
Smokes a little but the amenities make up for it.
Only two previous owners, very great women.
Come and kick the tires.
Two tone, white with a gray top.
Seeking a new woman owner who knows how to drive a classic!
Please put "classic" in your title for reply.
Thanks
PS. This car is at church every Sunday so if that is a problem with you, this car is not for you."

I found this exact ad on Craigslist after the fireworks faded away on July Fourth. I cannot imagine my mother finding a friend on

Craigslist. She was a cautious woman who lived a safe suburban life. Risk-taking was for others. She had stability and independence.

So did I, but I was bored. I wrote back.

"Love your ad.

I suppose I'd be a 1949 classic roadster.

Motor hums unless it hesitates. Transmission and gears probably need a road test.

Has never smoked.

Original owner.

Isn't kicking the tires painful?

Two tone, white with a reddish brown top

This classic roadster could be parked next to yours on Sunday.

Our roads aren't perfectly parallel. Might make life interesting.=) If anything piques your interest, feel free to write back."

We exchanged a couple more e-mails before he called. He was easy to talk to, sounded trustworthy, and my internal voice said, how long since you've been out to dinner with a man?

I'd had Chinese takeout with a platonic friend who died a year earlier from pancreatic cancer. I never told him my secret – I'd never had a boyfriend. I didn't say anything, and he never asked.

My 1944 Classic Roadster did, though. We went out for breakfast before driving up the coast on our second date. We'd already established that he was a two-time widower looking for a third wife, and I'd never been married. We were sitting in his Mazda, and he was lowering the top when he asked, "Have you ever had sexual relations?"

I shook my head. "No." It came out easily. I'd found a man who would ask the questions that would help me tell my truths and wouldn't judge me when I did.

Over the course of the next few weeks he got specific about why he wanted to be married and what he was looking for. He wanted the support of a good woman. Appearance was not a critical factor.

I wanted a relationship with an honest, loving man who would accept me as I am. We never dwelled on each other's flaws. He knows the importance of saying, "I love you," and so do I. I've seen the movie *The Craigslist Killer*, but Philip Markoff is not Richard Brown. Richard doesn't hide anything. We'd known each other for six weeks when he asked if I'd be willing to take his second wife's wedding ring as an engagement ring. I told him we needed to know each other better before we talked about getting married, but inside I glowed. He was in the midst of hard times, so I convinced myself to think of the ring as a family heirloom.

Although my mother could have remarried, she lived out her life with only a daughter to care for her. Even if she had known about internet dating, she could never had said yes to a man she met on Craigslist after seven months. But I did.

We were married in a wedding chapel in Reno on February 17, 2012. Richard bought me my own ring when he could. He makes me feel valued and loved every day.

B. Lynn Goodwin is the owner of Writer Advice, www.writeradvice.com, and the author of You Want Me to Do WHAT? Journaling for Caregivers *(Tate Publishing) and* Talent *(Eternal Press). She's published a memoir,* Never Too Late, *about getting married for the first time at 62.*

> *Owning our story can be hard but not nearly*
> *as difficult as spending our lives*
> *running from it.*[20]
>
> — BRENÉ BROWN,
> *The Gifts of Imperfection*

Nancy Neal Yeend

LIFE IS FOR THE BIRDS
Research on Robben Island

Nancy Neal Yeend, Robben Island, 2012

When I turned 68, my life seemed normal – I worked fulltime, volunteered in the community and attempted to learn how to master watercolors. Then my husband died and I was suddenly on my own: Children were grown and scattered throughout the country, and the only remaining pet was a 15-year-old cockatiel. As I began to adjust to this new circumstance, I realized that the potential for other changes in my life was endless, and so I began to consider all the things that could be explored. Since I volunteered at a wildlife rescue center and a local humane society, I naturally thought of animals.

So at age 69 I volunteered to help with a research project in South Africa, gathering data on, of all things, penguins! There is a large population of South African penguins living a half-mile off Capetown on Robben Island. In 2000 an oil tanker sank in the channel between the island and Capetown, and the penguin population appears to still be suffering the consequences.

Who could have imagined that at my age, with a replaced hip, I would be crawling on my stomach through the brush catching and then weighing and measuring penguins? More important in South Africa, and on the very island where Nelson Mandela had been held prisoner for so many years.

The Dutch initially settled Robben Island in the 1600s as a leper colony, and it is now a UNESCO World Heritage site. Visitors are escorted off the ferry, loaded onto buses and taken a few hundred yards for tours of the infamous prison – oblivious to the fact that the island has one of the largest penguin colonies in Africa.

The nonprofit Earthwatch sponsors a wide variety of research projects around the world by having volunteers pay to participate. Three of us joined the University of Capetown researcher and assistant for this project. While volunteering we stayed in a small house that originally was occupied by one of the prison guards. We each prepared our own breakfast and lunch, and cooking dinner was a shared effort. My biggest challenge in the food department was learning to cook ostrich, an apparent staple in the local diet.

Violent storms and strong currents are not uncommon in this region, and many ships have sunk in the channel between Robben Island and Capetown.

During my visit, a sunken ship became dislodged from a submerged ledge, broke apart and began seeping oil. We helped rescue more than 250 oiled penguins and transported them to Capetown for cleaning, rehabilitation and hopefully later release. In addition to rescuing the oiled birds, we had to inventory nests, identify chicks that lost an oiled parent, and transport those young birds to the rescue center to be raised until they could survive on their own.

Field conditions required a lot of walking and crawling. Even wading through the nearly five-foot-tall wild mustard required constant vigilance. The long mustard stalks could wrap around your boots and trip you, or you might encounter some unexpected creatures, including snakes.

Taking a risk, trying something extremely unfamiliar and voluntarily leaving your comfort zone are not traits of most 70-year-olds, and it is a missed discovery opportunity.

Nancy Neal Yeend is a mediator handling business disputes. She also serves on appellate mediation panels, mediates Americans With Disabilities Act disputes and teaches at the National Judicial College.

Mary Jo Lazear

THAT PINCH ON THE CHEEK
First marriage – at 71

There I was in June 2014 at my fiftieth college reunion celebrating 50 years as a successful professional and being grateful for the college education that had prepared me to be one. I was also celebrating my first marriage at the age of 71. On the other hand, many of my closest friends were celebrating 50 years of marriage because they had married immediately after graduation. I, obviously, did not.

Everyone clapped and cheered when it was announced at the reunion's banquet that I had just (or was it finally?) married for the first time. What an achievement, *non!* That is not say that I am not thrilled to have met "Mr. Right." He is a great guy, and we are extremely well suited. At this age and stage, ours is a marriage based on commitment, maturity, experience, and lots of love. We are both still working and enjoying it.

I vividly remember my relatives pinching me on the cheek at family weddings and saying with hope, "You're next, dear." I am certain I disappointed them. I always had the feeling that my very own dear mother did not consider me to be a complete person because I wasn't "settled" (her word). Unfortunately, she did not live to see me get married (and become complete, I guess). My mother's best friend, who is 97, came to the wedding. She assured me that she had come to represent my mother and that my mother was "looking down" with great pleasure.

I have had a long and rewarding career. I have spent my life advocating for the rights of women, first as a Planned Parenthood director, and subsequently as the reproductive health officer in the Europe and Eurasia bureau of USAID. I continue to do so.

I have traveled the world, sometimes alone (I have been to 51 countries), for either work or pleasure. I have felt that there is nothing I cannot do by myself or for myself. Certainly no one I know has ever spent time in Uzbekistan, or Azerbaijan, or Bangladesh as I have. My mother, on the other hand, did not like to travel. No matter where I went, even if I was spending some time in Paris, she would ask, "How far are you from Iraq?" Once, when we were on a train from Italy to France, I remarked how beautiful the hills were. She said, "Yes, but not as beautiful as our hills in Pittsburgh." To her credit, she loved just staying in her hometown.

I look back on my life with great pleasure. I have wonderful memories and, as Edith Piaf might have said, "Regrets, *je n'en ai pas*"!

One could say that Mary Jo Lazear gives true meaning to the word "detailist." Evidence her joy in remembering accent marks in the French language (she used to teach French). Mary Jo loves to organize parties and events down to the most minute detail. She thoroughly enjoys analyzing and creating recipes, paying attention to every grain of salt or sugar. Every detail in preparation for her journeys around the world presents an exciting challenge.

**Mary Jo Lazear and her husband,
Richard Karp, at their wedding,
Boston, Massachusetts, 2014**

Diana Kopp McDonough

My Second Life –
Global Grandmothers

Creating a nonprofit to aid children worldwide

I've always been a person of conscience – my father was a minister from a family where seven of the eight kids were ministers or missionaries. My grandmother pinned a world map to the dining room wall dotted with the location of missionaries we were praying for.

My religious paradigm of the universe changed after college, but planted forever in my psyche was a need to make a difference in the world.

In mid-life I married (twice, and now widowed), had two daughters, and worked full-time as a school attorney. In short, I was occupied!

In 2000, 55 years of age, I began to tire of 50-hour workweeks with my law firm, became of counsel (maintaining a relationship with the firm but not working as many hours), took a breath, and looked up.

With a little time and energy to focus beyond the four walls of my life, I realized that the world was still out there and that many of my fellow human beings suffered, starved, and helplessly watched their children do the same. I hadn't developed a satisfactory framework to respond to these needs. I didn't like the bad taste impulsive giving left in my mouth – but I liked not helping even less.

Then my first granddaughter was born. I couldn't believe how she captivated me – so perfect in each detail, so fragile – and so promising! But I was bothered too – by how much she enjoyed when so many children in the world had so little. By an accident of fate my granddaughter was born into a loving family in one of the world's richest countries while an equally deserving baby with loving parents was born into poverty and privation. How unfair the world seemed – and how little I was doing about it!

That was when I conceived of Global Grandmothers. The basic idea was simple – give to a child in need when you give to a grandchild – linked giving. Let the world's children benefit from the pooled generosity of caring grandmothers.

A simple method, I thought, would be to establish a website where grandmothers – and other caring individuals – could register their commitment to linked giving, keep track of that commitment, and contribute to organizations effective in supporting children worldwide. Maybe I could also make my grandchild aware of that linked gift, and global need, at the same time. Global Grandmothers would not seek funds for itself. Instead, it would be a conduit. It would generate commitment and facilitate giving to child-centered charities. I purchased two web domains.

On August 23, 2009, I read the *New York Times Magazine* article "Why Women's Rights Are the Cause of Our Time" by Nicholas D. Kristof and Sheryl WuDunn. The article announced the Half the Sky Contest asking readers to write about their efforts to address women's and girls' issues worldwide. My husband encouraged me to apply, and I got up my nerve. Although I didn't win, that application got me moving. I engaged others in the project and we got going.

By April 2010 Global Grandmothers was incorporated, by October it received federal tax-exempt status, and our website went live on January 18, 2011.

Now it is 2014 and Global Grandmothers boasts 100 members. Most are in California, but we have more than ten in other states, one in the District of Columbia and two in other countries. The latest Kristof/ WuDunn book, *A Path Appears,* includes a quote from our website!

But we're looking for that viral moment when we will become the standard in every household. Which of us can't afford to share a little when we give a gift to someone we love?

And as the ever health-conscious senior generation, we don't want to forget that giving contributes to happiness and longevity!

Diana McDonough is a proud California native, a graduate of Lynwood High School. As a scholarship student she took the Greyhound bus to begin as a freshman at Smith College, where she graduated in 1966. She later got a master's degree in history and secondary teaching credential from UC Berkeley. Ten years later, Diana went to Loyola of Los Angeles Law School, passed the California

Bar, and worked as an attorney representing school districts for 30 years. She has two children, three stepchildren, and eight grandchildren and now lives in the San Francisco Bay Area. Check out Global Grandmothers at www.globalgrandmothers.org.

**Diana Kopp McDonough and her granddaughter, Maddie,
at home, 2014**

The life you have led doesn't need to be the only life you have.[21]
— ANNA QUINDLEN,
"Anna Quindlen quotes"

UNPACKING MY BAGS
IN ANOTHER LOCALE

Ten or fifteen years ago normal people in their fifties, sixties, and seventies didn't go hiking in the Rocky Mountains or learn to paddle a sea kayak off the coast of New Zealand. They didn't sell their houses to buy a van and camp around Europe or stay with a family in Japan. That was for kids. Most Americans believed that once you hit fifty, it was downhill into retirement and old age. Maybe there'd be a bus tour or two along the way, with fellow travelers shouting for the guide to turn up the microphone. But if you were a widow or had a non-traveling spouse, the only acceptable vacation was a week with Aunt Thelma or your grown children...[22]

— MARCIA SCHNEDLER,
The Seasoned Traveler

Agnes Riedmann

MOVING/CAMPING ON

That first solo trip

In 1994, at age 51, I wedged all my belongings into my Nissan Sentra and drove from Omaha to Oakland, where I'd begin a new life. I took a royal blue tent that I'd bought and carried with me since shortly after the end of my marriage. In the prior two years I'd camped Nebraska, Minnesota, Montana, Colorado, Arizona and New Mexico. Once settled in California, I'd go on to camp in much of that state and western Canada. I've now camped all along the Columbia River; crawled the Pacific coast, Astoria to San Francisco; and found (some) company in the few campsites along Nevada's Highway 50, dubbed loneliest in the world.

To celebrate the millennium, I bought a 1988 Westphalia. I loved that Westy, but in the six years I had it I acquired too many tow-truck photos. Now I have a Ford campervan, bought used off a lot. It had few miles because, as the salesperson kept repeating, the former own-ers were old. Last June my twenty-year-old granddaughter and I drove it to Tok, Alaska, and back with just a bit of cheating on the Alaska Marine Highway ferry. Despite having the van, I still carry and often put up my tent. It's airy and keeps me grounded, pun not intended.

My first camping trip I owe to my former husband, Bill, who sug-gested in July, 1964, that we pack sleeping mats and pancake mix into our Chevy and drive to western Nebraska, where afternoons it was 105 and nights it might get down to 80. We tented by an icy stream, its current recently having been Colorado snow pack. I spent the first afternoon hopping into the water to beat the heat, then vaulting onto the bank because my icy ankles burned.

Bill buckled first, said it's just too hot and what do you say we bag it. We did. We didn't camp after that, and I didn't miss it. But that trip had sparked in me a love for Nebraska topography.

Sometime following a grey morning 19 years later, when I watched Bill move his things from our family home, after I'd gazed seasons out the window, I bought a royal blue tent, a two-person dome that comfortably sleeps one and a half. I wouldn't choose that color again; it's not cool. But you can find it easily in a campground. The evening I purchased it, I set it up in the living room, managing to get all three-fiberglass poles in place before morning. Nevertheless, I didn't use that tent for 10 years. Just drove it around in my trunk.

The first place where I spent the night in that tent was the Nebraska National Forest along the Loup River. I was on my way back to

Agnes Riedmann, Crocker Museum, Sacramento, California, 2013

Omaha from the South Dakota Badlands. In three months I'd be 50. The road wound me to the modest memorial cemetery. A Native American teen appeared on a bicycle too small for him. "You want to buy some earrings?" His father had made them at the family table. I bought yellow porcupine-quill hoops. Having breathed an open and opening landscape all day, I just couldn't pinch myself into a right-angled motel room. Besides, having lain in my trunk for nearly ten years, my tent had grown a face. The eyes sometimes caught mine when I opened the hatch: "Try me, I'll make you happy all night," they said. "It's not that hard to get me up either."

Still not sure whether I was really going to camp, I turned into the forest. It was late afternoon. It hadn't been dark on the highway, but it was pretty shadowy in this tall-treed campground. Now I was growing more hesitant about tenting. I could drive on toward Broken Bow, maybe, find a Holiday Inn, read a free *USA Today*. But Tent said, "You'd quit *now*?" Thankfully I didn't.

In 1994, Agnes Riedmann drove her stuff (eventually she used the word moved) from Omaha to the San Francisco Bay Area. After teaching part-time at Diablo Valley College, Agnes landed a tenure-track position at CSU Stanislaus in California, where she is now a semi-retired sociology professor. Agnes has two children: Beth and Bill, and three grandchildren: Natalie, 21, Alex, 12, and Livia, 11. Everyone in the family likes to travel.

Pam McNeilly

WALLS

Road trips to the same location – years apart

Wall, South Dakota, 1970

Zeke and I got a ride here from St. Paul, the first leg of our journey hitchhiking to California. Wall is a tourist stop on a desolate stretch of Interstate 90. Its few residents staff the cafe and the souvenir shops and live in small box houses dotting the two other streets in this town. An incongruous tiny community library built of stone anchors the end of the street.

I had been working as a cabin girl at a resort in northern Minnesota until summer's end. I fell in lust with Zeke, the maintenance man, who was my age and traveling around the country to avoid the draft. He wanted to head to Oregon after the resort job and wanted me to come with him. So I dropped out of college and we made our way to the interstate with our duffel bags, one sleeping bag between us. How can I ever tell my mother? Perhaps I'll leave out the sleeping arrangements, I think as we stand on the freeway entrance ramp, waiting for our next ride.

Wall, South Dakota, 1973

John and I stop here for a dose of kitsch and a piece of pie. I'd like to spend more time perusing the trinkets and cedar boxes reminiscent of the 1940s, but John wants to get on the road, so we leave. He had gotten busted for furnishing marijuana, and as soon as his probation ended we flew Icelandic Airlines to Europe and bought a VW bus to drive and live in during the five months we spent there. We shipped the bus to New Jersey and now we are driving it back home to California.

The tiny library is still here and reminds me of my adventure with Zeke. He took good care of me on that trip, which ended when we parted ways in Berkeley. John, too, takes good care of me, making sure we have regular meals and a safe place to park the bus each night – still our home until we get back.

Wall, South Dakota, 2014

Maria and I park the SUV on Main Street in front of the little stone library. I am pleased it still stands, some sort of intellectual opportunity for residents of this isolated town.

I've had a 30-year teaching career and a 25-year relationship with a man who died and left me a large house but no money. I learned to use a Sawzall and a drill and a weed whacker and how to repair irrigation systems and clean gutters.

When I retired, my mother died. I gave away most of her things and stored what I wanted to keep, with the intention of returning to drive them back home. My friend Maria, also retired, did not want me to drive from Arkansas to California alone. Her husband recently has habituated to her preparing meals and doing the shopping and the laundry. So this was an opportunity for him to remember how to take care of himself and for Maria and me to have an adventure.

We flew to Arkansas and loaded the stored items into a rented SUV. We stopped at my mother's grave, where I buried the last remnants of her fears and her anger, and we began to drive.

We had negotiated an itinerary that took us north through Missouri, Kansas, Iowa, Nebraska, then west through South Dakota. On the way to the Black Hills, it seemed apt to visit Wall before heading to Mt. Rushmore.

That tiny stone library appears the same as it was 40 years earlier, but I have changed immeasurably.

We buy souvenir hoodies for our collections and continue driving. After viewing Mt. Rushmore, we travel through Deadwood to Sundance, to Cody, then south on narrow roads across high desert plains to Salt Lake City, where we turn west again toward home in California.

On this trip we take good care of ourselves. We make frequent stops to stretch muscles stiff from sitting; we take turns driving, and we stay in good hotels. There are tornado warnings in Kansas, thunderstorms in the Black Hills, sleet and snow through the Big Horn Mountains, dust devils in the salt flats. We navigate the challenges together with aplomb and finally unload the truck at my home, celebrating the victories of our 3,000-mile road trip.

Pam McNeilly is a Thursday's Child, and has always had far to go. She grew up in small-town Minnesota, the daughter of a minister and a teacher, and escaped at the earliest opportunity.

Pam McNeilly at home, 2015

You do not travel if you are afraid of the unknown, you travel for the unknown, that reveals you with yourself.[23]

— ELLA MAILLART,
"Ella Maillart Quotes"

Sharon Dirlam

PEACE CORPS, RUSSIAN FAR EAST, 1996-98

Teaching English

The morning gossip in the cafeteria involved Lisa and Brian, who spent the night together in a tent after Lisa's roommate complained that she didn't join the Peace Corps to sleep in the same room with a sex-crazed couple.

John, 62, and I, 56, began to suspect that our Peace Corps adventure wouldn't be quite the same as that of the other trainees, most of whom were fresh out of college.

Those first weeks of training as volunteers to the Russian Far East took place in a remote corner of West Virginia between the village of Athens and a funky bar called The Last Resort. It was a fitting milieu to prepare us for the remote assignments we hoped we were headed for.

Russia was being stubborn about issuing visas to us, so those first weeks were filled with uncertainty. The young people had their hearts set on adventure, while our minds were preoccupied with the fact that our house was already rented out and our careers were on hold. But at last, our visas came through and we piled onto buses, planes and trains to get to our Russian training town of Ussuriisk.

John and I crowded each other on a fold-out couch in the small apartment of Nadezhda, an energetic factory guard. Nadezhda worked at night, gardened at her dacha, and had enough canned vegetables on hand to last a decade. Her unemployed son Andrei came by frequently, usually drunk, and sometimes not alone. Andrei was helpful in teaching us Russian phrases, such as "Don't tell Mama" and "Please close the door."

When training ended, we were sent to Birobidjan, capital of the Jewish Autonomous Region, to teach English to teachers of English.

We arrived by train at dawn and were met by swarms of a trillion mosquitoes. (Birobidjan was built on a swampland a century ago.) Our

Sharon Dirlam, Birobidjan, 1997

apartment wasn't quite ready – no cupboards, no stove, no bedding. But an afternoon banquet, complete with caviar and vodka, welcomed us.

Many of our fellow teachers had never heard a native speaker of English, so mostly they taught reading and writing. They had some reservations about us. I once corrected a teacher's pronunciation and she replied, "I'm speaking British English, not American."

Another problem was that the Russian teachers of English had evolved their own complicated version of English grammar, which the students all had to memorize. We decided it wasn't our place to challenge their authority.

My classes, then, focused on speaking and listening. Critical thinking wasn't being taught either, as far as I could tell; rather, teachers lectured students on what they should understand. When I asked a student, "What is this character's motivation?" he replied, confused, "What do you want me to say?"

I considered it a great success when several students got involved in a lively debate about the motives of the characters in "The Great Gatsby," their favorite American novel (and the only complete American novel available in classroom sets).

By the end of our two years, John and I had been invited to demonstrate our teaching methods all around the region and we spent the last week having our voices taped reading their English textbooks aloud.

I liked shopping in the *rinok* (open-air market) and riding the clunky old buses that gave excellent service all around town and beyond.

I was both glad and heartbroken to visit the local orphanage. The children eagerly hung on to me and proudly showed off their neat cots and their little box of clothes. Older Russians who'd once lived there returned often to visit. Teachers and children alike cleaned the buildings and tended the gardens that provided most of their food.

Winter taught us about Russian endurance; daytime temperatures are generally zero to twenty degrees above. When you shop in the *rinok* or stand waiting for a bus, winter is especially hard.

We made friends, several of whom are still in touch. My Russian language skills, the little I ever had, have faded, but the love remains strong for the people who invited us to their apartments and shared their gossip, explained their culture and opened their hearts.

Sharon Dirlam wrote a memoir, Beyond Siberia: Two Years in a Forgotten Place, *about serving in the Peace Corps in Birobidjan. She has a Master's Internationalist degree from the School for International Training in Brattleboro, Vermont, a bachelor's degree from Antioch University, and was a Professional Journalism Fellow at Stanford University. She has worked as an editor and staff writer at newspapers in Indiana, Colorado, New Hampshire, and California, including the* Santa Barbara News-Press *and the* Los Angeles Times.

Sharon Dirlam at home, 2014

Geri Thayer

WHO CLIMBS MT. KILIMANJARO AS A SENIOR CITIZEN?

The author did…and didn't whine

Geri Thayer, 1998

So, I was over 60, still skiing, hiking and roller blading. My husband was in the hospital recovering from cancer surgery and we received an invitation from one of his corporate clients to climb Mt. Kilimanjaro with a small group of executives from around the world, led by Outward Bound.

I had just finished reading Michael Crichton's book *Travels* with a chapter on his ascent of the mountain, which had left me with no desire to ever go there. I took the invitation to the hospital and gave it to Don saying, "Too bad we can't do this." He replied, "Why not?" The doctor was in the room and I handed him the invite and commented that it was in six weeks and I was sure the doctor would not want him to go. The doctor immediately said that Don should be fine by then. When the physical form arrived, I put down every knee surgery and ailment I could think of, while Don filled his out honestly.

The company called and asked if I was really able to do this…I was, but not very enthusiastic. I also realized after reading the list of people on the trip that we were the oldest of the group. I had read that if you did not want to go to the top, you could stop at 15,000 feet and do alternate hikes while the rest of the group went on. I was thinking that was a great option until my daughter called as we were leaving and said she had been thinking about my plan and went on to say, "Mom, you have only one shot at this...so give it your BEST and go for it. Also, do me a favor...Don't whine!"

Five weeks after receiving the invite we were off to Nairobi where we met the group and our Outward Bound leaders while sitting helter skelter on the grass at the Nairobi Country Club. The leader of OB said "Let's all sit in a circle so no one is at the head." Not one of the big executives moved. They were all used to being at the head. Soon we were off in small planes to the OB camp at the base of the mountain. I was put on a plane with a man from England (head of the Tate Museum), a developer from India, another from Mexico, a woman in her prayer shawl from Tibet, a French lady and one person from Outward Bound. Our pilot was used to flying for one of the African Airlines and not used to small planes. When we got to the mountain, the OB person helped him find the runway and, rather than doing a fly-by to check it out, he landed...touching down just at the end of the runway, and we went hurtling off down a hill, hitting bushes. The wing was torn off and we came to a stop at a big tree that would have flipped the plane. The pilot yelled that we should get out quickly as there was gas everywhere, and both pilots disappeared out the front door. I thought they would open our door but, when they did not, I quickly ran to the back, opened the door, let down the stairs and jumped out, followed by the others. My husband had a Cessna and I knew how to do this.

An auspicious start to the hike. At OB camp they taught us to put up tents, pack our food, etc. Finally we took off and started the slow march up the mountain. At the end of the first day it took us so long to put up the tents that the next nights, OB and the porters had them up and waiting for us. By the end of the third day, we were at 15,000 feet, and I knew that I did not want to stay there as we were so dirty and just to sit and wait for the others seemed pointless. If we had been able to head down to a hotel and shower I might have gone, but that was not an option. We went to our tents early as we got up at midnight, and with headlamps started the trek to the top. There was a fast group and a slow group...Don was well in the lead of the faster group and I was at the end of fast group. It was all scree...and for every two steps forward you slid back one. I managed not to whine, but I did cry to myself. The lack of oxygen was noticeable and the chocolate bars I had stashed in my jacket tasted like sawdust. When we finally made it, Outward Bound was there to congratulate us and take photos. All I wanted to do was start down as I was worried about the scree and sliding. It turned out that the scree part was fun, you dug in your heel and slid in total control. Our group walked 15 hours that day and the slow group walked 18 hours. The reward was being able to tell my daughter that I did it!

Geri Thayer is now 77, still hiking, swimming, skiing, traveling but she finds she is not able to get up as easily when she falls on the slopes or gets out of a scull or kayak by herself, and her legs will not stop shaking on a paddle board. What is that all about? Some of her 12 grandchildren are growing up and becoming interesting individuals, others are still young and precious, and there are a lot of reasons to keep in good shape and to keep going.

The impulse to travel is one of the hopeful symptoms of life.[24]
— AGNES REPPLIER,
Times and Tendencies

Barbara Nube Roose

THE TIMELY DEATH OF A MOTTO

Setting up a cottage – in Bolivia

What was I doing crawling behind a man through thick subtropical underbrush? I was trying to be nonchalant about the unfamiliar creepy crawling creatures and was relieved when we came to a tree and I was able to stand and look around. We were checking the boundaries of the land. Weeds covered everything except the boulders.

A teacher and I had taken children on their first trip to the countryside and he had suggested that I buy land. I had lived in Bolivia for 23 years. My youngest son had just left to study in the States. I had turned 55 and was open to changes. But to buy land sounded crazy.

The bee the teacher put in my bonnet refused to leave. I looked at land and fell in love with this site. It had lain fallow in a coffee and citrus region of small farms interspersed with isolated homes of La Paz residents appropriately called Pankarani (Place of Flowers). With 30 households, Pankarani had been part of a hacienda that was subdivided by the 1955 Land Reform.

I stood at the entrance to an acre and a half at an elevation of 5,000 feet. A dirt road led to Coroico, with 10,000 inhabitants the largest town in Nor Yungas Province in Western Bolivia. Behind me was a majestic mountain, below a meandering river. Several of Cordillera Real's snow-capped peaks were visible in the distance. The view, the flowers and the birdsong bewitched me. There were no neighbors, no electricity, no telephone lines and not even a connection to the water tank a quarter mile away. But we had found water trickling between the roots of a walnut tree!

I had grown up under my mother's motto "Don't buy a home. Travel and buy books; nobody can destroy that!" That made sense to my mother, who had survived two world wars in Germany and as a Jew had lost family members, her profession, her belongings and almost her life. But after living in rentals for almost half a century, I had had enough. Motto or no motto, I had bought an apartment in La

Paz. Now I saw an opportunity to live in nature for part of each month.

My mother is no longer alive. I am a Holocaust survivor who became a social worker in Bolivia. I am divorced and have three sons. I like challenges. My mother's example in keeping true to her convictions is important. She demonstrated that drastic change is possible when she fulfilled her dream to become a painter after having been a physical therapist.

I had broken her motto once; it was easier the second time. I bought the land and named it Marianne in my mother's honor.

Men from the area built three small cottages and many stone walls. They captured water from the spring by the tree for a small swimming pool. We planted citrus trees and transplanted endangered fern trees and orchids from pristine areas being turned into roads. I led occasional workshops and retreats, took walks, gardened, read, drew and wrote to understand the effects of traumas.

I was elected the treasurer of the local farmers' union. We dealt with public entities and built a water connection to every plot in Pankarani. I rushed to La Paz after every 10-day stay to earn the money to continue.

I weathered catastrophes when one cottage had to be rebuilt after being destroyed by termites, roots plugged up sewage pipes, and a main retaining wall collapsed. I had to hire a permanent caretaker after I was robbed.

We harvested bananas, avocados, oranges, tangerines and coffee beans. I learned that by clapping my hands, I could stop a new queen bee flying with her swarm from settling on my land. And that a big flock of birds, which returns at dusk to its favorite tree, takes just as long to settle down as toddlers who ask for one more story to be read at bedtime.

I was 70 when I moved to California in 2008 to join two of my sons and their families. I had expected to die in Bolivia, but instead I embarked upon the unknown once more. This time it is to learn the art and craft of being a grandmother and writer, which reminds me of crawling through underbrush without knowing what I'll come upon.

Barbara Nube Roose was born in Germany, where she survived the Holocaust. Her early immigrant years in Venezuela, her later studies in the U.S., her marriage, and the births of two sons in the States during the '60s affirmed a desire to return to South America. She worked as a community organizer and later as a therapist in Bolivia for 39 years, where she also had her third son.

Barbara Nube Roose, Pankarani, Bolivia, 2007

*You have set sail on another ocean without star
or compass going where the arguement (sic) leads
shattering the certainties of centuries.*[25]

— JANET KALVEN,
"Respectable Outlaw"

REALIZING A DREAM

If your dreams do not scare you, they are not big enough.[26]
— ELLEN JOHNSON SIRLEAF,
Commencement Address, Harvard University

Elizabeth Chafcouloff

SPEECH THERAPY CAMBODIA

In her late 60s, the author starts a non-profit

November, 2013: Sovith was desperate. His 85-year old father had been hospitalized in Phnom Penh, Cambodia, after a stroke and could not eat because he could not swallow. He was losing weight every day and getting weaker. The family began making plans for a funeral.

A very tech-savvy guy, Sovith searched the internet and discovered that speech therapists could treat swallowing problems. He googled "speech therapy" and "Cambodia" and he found...me. How did I get here? Why Cambodia?

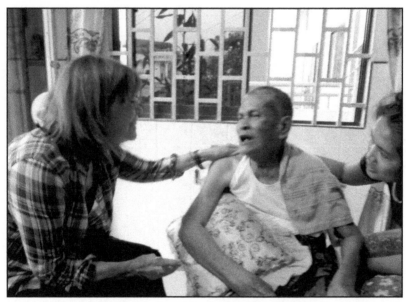

Elizabeth Chafcouloff and Sovith's father, Cambodia, 2013

Flashback 25 years to the late 1980s. I was an ESL teacher, had taught in Japan, and was teaching international refugee and immigrant populations in San Francisco.

At that time, a huge surge of Cambodian refugees had come to the United States, including San Francisco. These people had spent 10

years in refugee camps in Thailand following the Khmer Rouge genocide from 1975 to 1979. Many were not literate even in their native
language.

In stepped the Refugee Women's Program, a volunteer organization in San Francisco. I became a volunteer literacy teacher with the
program, tutoring Cambodian women in their homes. I became very
attached to them and to their culture.

The years passed. I changed careers, finishing a graduate degree
in speech pathology in 2002 at age 56. I began practicing as a specialist in speech and swallowing treatment for adults and the elderly.
Swallowing therapy has become a very important part of the speech
pathologist's practice. Many people suffering from neurological dis-
orders die from pneumonia and malnutrition caused by swallowing
problems. But the right therapy techniques can help. The dilemma of
Sovith's father is not unique.

I didn't travel to Cambodia until 2008. Once there, I was fascinated to find a million and one NGOs, most with a mission to serve
the undereducated and others at risk. I thought I would like to volunteer my services in Cambodia once I retired. For the next five years,
I networked to explore this possibility. I must have corresponded
with nearly 100 individuals and organizations during that period.
Unfortunately, I found that there were very few speech therapy services in Cambodia, and none at all for adults.

In 2013, back in Cambodia, I met with some of the people I had
corresponded with – educators, health care workers, audiologists,
university administrators. I asked them, "How can we bring speech
therapy to Cambodia?"

There is a saying in Cambodia that there is always one woman in
a village – not the most powerful woman, but someone that everyone
listens to. One of my contacts was a nurse who works at a large public
hospital in Phnom Penh, the Russian Hospital. Her name is Thavry
and she was this woman. Thavry spoke about me to the deputy director of the hospital, and a few months later, I was invited to volunteer.

A friend in California suggested that I start a nonprofit corpora-
tion to fund my project in Cambodia, and this I did. Speech Therapy
Cambodia was incorporated as a nonprofit charity in late 2013.

In early 2014, I returned to Cambodia once more and started swallowing therapy training for four neurologists at the Russian Hospital. They are a young, smart, and very enthusiastic group, very eager to help their patients. One doctor, Nara, told me, "Yes, I saw swallowing therapy when I was studying in France, but we don't know how to do this here!"

We have plans to organize a free speech and language clinic for the poor (to start in the winter of 2014) and to expand services to other hospitals. Eventually the goal would be to have the government agree to a university degree in speech language pathology for Cambodians.

I'll be traveling to Cambodia for the next five years, twice a year, for several months at a time to continue training until we can establish a sustainable program run by Cambodians, the ultimate goal.

I saw Sovith's father several times in 2013-14. He is still with us! The family is managing his treatment using techniques I taught them. I heard just lately that he is now able to eat noodles again!

Betsy Chafcouloff is a 68-year-old speech and language pathologist. She has been traveling on and off for almost 50 years, and is particularly drawn to working with people in Asia. Betsy thought she would retire and read and walk and have lunch with friends and exercise more, but she was more driven than she had imagined. She didn't think that she would start a nonprofit, but "it kind of took on a life of its own!" For more information on the project see www.speechtherapycambodia.org.

Elizabeth Chafcouloff and a hospital team, Cambodia, 2014

Susanna Solomon

THE PE EXAM

Despite the naysayers, the author became
an electrical engineer

"What are you doing?" the white-haired man asked. His wife, sitting beside him, clicked her purse open.

Four books were spread out on a table in front of me, along with binders and a cheat sheet. We were at a Red Lion hotel in Sacramento, the night before my PE exam.

"Studying," I said. Years before, married to an alcoholic, I had seen engineering as a ticket out and went back to school. Now, at forty-one, working in a decent job, divorced, and starting my career late, I wanted to get my license.

"Studying for what?"

"My PE exam," I said.

"PE as in physical education? They have exams for that?"

"Uh, no. Professional engineer."

"For you?"

"Yes, yes, of course for me," I answered. "I'm an engineer."

He snorted.

It had taken me two years to get employment verification records and another two to get the five references the exam required. My bosses at the time had refused on both counts.

"Women can't become engineers," he said.

"But I am."

"Sir," I said. "I need to review my notes."

It was October. I'd spent the last six months studying – on top of a full-time job and raising my kids by myself. I had been the top student in my class for seven years. But his words still affected me. The eight-hour exam had a 22% pass rate.

"You'll never make it."

"Harold, leave the poor girl alone," Harold's wife said and they left.

He was right. I had no right to even try. I was a dunderhead. My notes looked like worms.

Shaken, I walked over to a pay phone and called my best friend. "Am I doing the right thing?" I asked.

"Of course," she answered.

Feeling encouraged, I packed all my notes and headed upstairs. A show about Marian Anderson was on TV. As she sang "Ave Maria" in front of the Lincoln Memorial in 1939 for 75,000 people, I wept. She was outside because the Daughters of the American Revolution had refused to let her sing in Constitution Hall. If she could do it, so could I.

The next morning I, along with 100 other hopefuls, lined up at Cal Expo in a driving rain waiting for admission. The exam was the hardest test I had ever taken. Thrice in the morning I didn't think I'd pass, and in the middle of the afternoon I almost gave up. Seven years of science and math, an eight-hour prep exam, and Harold's voice kept me in my seat. I walked out, ready to write a check for the next try.

Four months later I received a phone call from a friend who had taken the exam with me. He was at the license headquarters in Sacramento. I listened, prepared to congratulate him. "I wasn't on the list," he said, and was quiet a moment, "but you were."

I had passed.

Susanna Solomon in her office, Santa Rosa, California, 1996

Twenty-two years later, I gaze on that PE certificate on my wall that allowed me to open my own business fifteen years ago. People ask me, is it scary?

Scary, versus what? Being laughed at when I talked over the phone with potential bosses who asked me how old I was? Getting fired when I told the owner of the first company I worked for that my manager came in drunk every day and the next week found myself outside the door, without a job or severance? Scary versus the days when my next boss used to scream in my ear, I got a migraine headache and on the way home lost my lunch behind a bush on Lombard Street? Scary? Nah, it's not scary.

Nine months after I started my own business, I doubled my previous salary. The second year I made so much money I invested it. The third year I cut back my hours. I've had up years and down years, but I've never had a bad year. And I've never had anyone doubt who I am and what I do. The phone rings. I must be doing something right. When do I want to retire? At sixty-five? I'm not sure. I'm having too much fun.

Susanna Solomon is both an author and an electrical engineer. She has been an engineer for twenty-five years and a writer for longer than that. After many years of taking classes and workshops, she was asked to write a few short stories. Her short story collection, Point Reyes Sheriff's Calls, *was published in December 2013 by HD Media Press.* Point Reyes Sheriff's Calls *has been on the* Marin Independent Journal *bestseller list twice. She is at work on a novel. Susanna has lived in Marin County, California, for decades.*

Susanna Solomon, Marin County, 2013

Linda Slavin Kirby

No Regrets

Realizing a lifelong dream – a bacherlor's degree

I was raised in a comfortable Boston suburb by upper-middle class parents. Although both my parents were college-educated, we never discussed books or scientific discoveries or the problems of the world. Reading was not valued, and I do not remember being read to as a child. Dad was a successful businessman and worked hard to support us. Mom had been a dental hygienist before they married, but she had to quit because a working woman indicated that her husband was not able to support her. My parents naturally assumed that I would not work and would marry a man who would "support me in the style to which I had become accustomed."

After I graduated from high school, I went to a junior college (different from today's community colleges as I lived on campus in a dorm in another state.) Although I was a terrible student, I always liked learning. It stimulated me. It secretly bothered me that I did poorly. I never knew it was because I never learned how to learn.

Much to my parents' consternation, I was a rebellious sort and not about to let them dictate whom I would marry. At 21 I did marry and, although we had a great relationship, nine years and two daughters later we divorced.

After working at Harvard Business School, Brandeis University and as an administrative assistant to a lawyer, I realized I didn't like the rigidity of a 9 to 5 job. I wanted more flexibility and independence. I studied to become a certified court reporter and, following in my dad's footsteps, opened my own business. Poor dad didn't know whether to be proud or embarrassed.

I remarried, my girls were launched and, by my mid-50s I was getting oh-so-tired of sitting stone-faced in the courtroom recording verbatim testimony of who did or did not do whatever to whomever. I always had been fascinated by the language of the deaf, American Sign Language (ASL). Sign language interpreters mirrored what I was writing on my stenotype machine, except the words were being translated by flying, graceful hands and emotive faces.

At age 55 I enrolled in a two-year ASL program at my local community college. I loved it. I shuttered my business and became the court-access liaison for a nonprofit legal firm that represented hearing-impaired people. It was exhilarating to stay in law, the field I had come to love, but education had me in its grips.

Years before, my sage and prescient father-in-law had proclaimed, "You don't want to die with any regrets." But I DID have a regret. My lifelong dream was to get my bachelor's degree. I didn't do it when I was supposed to because I didn't think I was smart enough. That may have been true then, but it sure wasn't now. I talked with counselors who assured me that if I qualified academically, age would not be a problem. At age 63 I went back to community college to fulfill the university's prerequisites. I entered the University of California, Berkeley, at age 65 as a legal studies major. My first semester was

Linda Slavin Kirby at home, 2014
(Photo by Nancy Rubin)

daunting and intimidating.

My fellow students were 20 years younger than my own children. What was I doing here? Then I realized I did have something to offer – maturity and experience. I began to share with my classmates: my excitement when LBJ signed the Civil Rights Act of 1964; my struggle to have a safe abortion in 1971, two years before Roe v. Wade; my awe and respect for my political-activist disabled friends here in Berkeley who helped shape the Americans with Disabilities Act (ADA).

One of my fondest memories is the many students who said, "My mom would be so jealous. She always wanted to go back to school." I grinned and replied, "Tell her to call me!"

In 2009 at age 67 I graduated with my much-desired bachelor's degree. (And I just gotta throw in that during my spring break I successfully summited Mt. Kilimanjaro, 19,300 feet, at age 66!)

Now I have no regrets!

Linda Slavin Kirby continues to hike (although she's not climbing any more mountains), took her daughters on a three-week African safari to celebrate their "significant" birthdays, and recently returned to the world of tap dancing, which she had previously left.

Throw your dreams into space like a kite, and you do not know
what it will bring back, a new life, a new friend,
a new love, a new country.[27]

– ANAÏS NIN,
The Diary of Anaïs Nin, Volume 4

Susan Lundgren

MENDOCINO DREAMING

Finding the perfect place to live

Long before I retired, I began looking for the perfect place to live. Oakland had been good to me, but I knew I wanted a different, quieter, more picturesque life for my later decades. I looked everywhere I ventured, from Europe to Costa Rica and even in other parts of the U.S. I finally found what I was looking for, almost in my own backyard.

My childhood had included many trips to Fort Bragg. In fact, our family used to joke that we had relatives on every corner there. My aunt worked in Mendocino's general store, my uncles were lumberjacks and fishermen, and one relative owned a sheep ranch in Albion. But I never saw the area as one where I'd return to live.

Then one day I wandered through Mendocino's village and I knew instantly that this is what I had been hoping to find. Although I knew no one else in the area, I bought a house and packed my bags for the new life I'd chosen.

The part I've left out, however, is that I also left the man I love to be here.

Unlike my mother, I never chose marriage. There were proposals; I wasn't interested. My unhappy childhood and my feminism had sealed my fate. I never again wanted to be in a situation I couldn't easily leave, and neither did I want to deal with societal expectations surrounding marriage.

Prior to Phillip, I'd been unpartnered for many years. Nevertheless, within my first three weeks of knowing him I told him I didn't "do" marriage, and, by the way, I'd be moving to Mendocino. He took the risk, we lived happily in Oakland together for three years, and then I made my move. In spite of my great love for him, I left for the life that was calling me.

I breathe more freely here. I walk daily, I've become obsessed with birds, and I stop to smell the flowers and enjoy the views. I'm learning to paint, am active in politics and study groups, volunteer everywhere, belong to book clubs, take yoga and pilates, march under varying banners in local parades, and I even took acting classes for a while!

An unexpected pleasure here is that I'm also surrounded by women who are decades older than I. They're active artists, political leaders, and wonderful role models for aging and living the lives they've designed. I'm lucky to be able to call them my friends.

As for me and Phillip? We struggle with the miles between us. Our bond is strong but the separation is difficult. We each travel the seven hours round-trip between Oakland and Mendocino at least once each month, and we keep trying to figure out how to make our relationship work. I miss the daily intimacy of being with him, but Mendocino is the dream I chose, and although he loves it here, he also loves tall buildings and cement. Maybe he'll move here or maybe he won't. Maybe he'll buy a house closer and we'll rotate between our two residences. Or maybe we won't last, which would make me very sad.

As for my mother? She was married to my father for over 60 years, and she would never have left him or created a life distinctly separate from his. She wouldn't have risked security for the unknown, and she undoubtedly would not have approved of my choices. But I have no regrets. I'm happy here, I know this is where I need to be, and it's where I plan to stay.

Susan Lundgren worked as a counselor and instructor (women's studies, psychology and career classes) at Diablo Valley College for over thirty years. Her education includes a doctorate in education from the University of San Francisco. At the age of 66, she has now been living in Mendocino for just over four years.

Susan Lundgren at home, 2014

Sherry Lou Macgregor
On A Journey In a Canoe
Traveling by canoe is in the author's blood

The canoe named *Laxaynem* and crew, Puget Sound, 2012
(Photo by Charlene Dick)

I do not know how it came into my mind, but one day I knew I wanted to get into a Canoe and go on a Canoe Journey with my People. I was 64 years old and had never been in a Canoe. But this is exactly what I did. My People are the Jamestown S'Klallam of the House of Steteethlum, a Coast Salish Indian Tribe in Washington State. One of my S'Klallam friends told me, "The water calls to you." She is right.

To go on a Canoe Journey is a bit complicated. One factor is that I live in California and the Canoe Journeys take place in Washington State and British Columbia, Canada. Another is the requirements for participation: the practices and training and finally the Canoe Journey itself. For me this means moving close to Tribal lands for most of the summer. And for six consecutive summers, this is exactly what I did.

In the Pacific Northwest, Tribal Canoe Journeys occur each summer. We begin our Canoe Journey from our own Tribal lands with Tribes hosting us along the way. Anywhere from 30 to 60 Tribes participate, and in recent years there have been over 100 traditional Canoes at the final landing. After a day's journey we must ask formal permission to come ashore. The hosting Tribe then provides a big Feast for everyone. In the evenings there is often Singing, Drumming, Dancing and Story-telling. Early the next morning when the tides and weather conditions are just right, we get in our Canoe and paddle for another day. How many days a canoe is on the water depends on the distance between one's Tribal lands and that of the Final Host.

My first summer, in preparation for the Canoe Journey, I made my own Paddle from yellow cedar. It has a leaf-shaped blade that comes to a point at the tip. I painted a Sea-Bear on mine (part Bear and part Killer Whale), a protective image for a sea-going Paddle. I also acquired a traditional woven Cedar Hat to wear on the Canoe Journey.

Our dugout canoe is named *Laxaynem* after an Ancestor and is carved from a 500-year-old first-growth red cedar tree.

Paddling in this Canoe in a large body of water always makes me feel like a pin-prick in the Universe. It is humbling and exhilarating at the same time. It is like no other experience that I have ever had. There are days of great beauty and calmness and days of high waves and turbulence. Some days we hear singing from other Canoes but cannot see them or the land we pass because of the fog.

Other days when the sun shines, everything is crystal clear, even what is beneath us in the water: Jellyfish, Porpoises, Seals, Schools of Fish and once even a Gray Whale that swam under our Canoe.

One experiences the Unexpected on a Canoe Journey. It is as though the Water gives us Gifts. There is the strength you do not know you have to keep paddling hour after hour, the bond you have with the others in your Canoe, the Traditions that are observed or participated in and our connections with the Ancestors. The last is particularly important as the Canoe was how the Ancestors moved themselves and their belongings from place to place, the means with which they journeyed to social events, where they collected, hunted or fished for food and the vessel in which they might be placed when they died.

For me being in a Canoe on a Canoe Journey has informed me about myself and my Indian Culture. I am mentally and physically stronger than I ever imagined. I have the doggedness to keep pulling stroke after stroke. I have experienced fear and overcome it to arrive at our destination. I have learned an Ancient Etiquette that fosters respect for each other, especially the Elders. I have heard Myths and Stories and Songs that deeply resonate in my life. It has made me feel much closer to my Mother, my Grandmother and my Great-Grandmother, who endowed me with this rich Heritage. The Canoe Journeys have been much more than I ever originally imagined. Another S'Klallam friend said to me, "The first time you get in a Canoe you will know if it is in your Blood." And I knew. It was.

American Indian and Scottish, Sherry Lou Macgregor is an elder in the Jamestown S'Klallam Tribe. Each summer she is a "puller" in the tribe's canoe on Tribal Canoe Journeys. Her experiences and observations on these Canoe Journeys have inspired her to document the history of Pacific Northwest Coast Indian Canoe Cultures. She is currently writing a book on this subject. In 2012 she published Beyond Hearth and Home: Women in the Public Sphere in Neo-Assyrian Society.

Sherry Lou Macgregor, Washington State, 2009
(Photo by Betty Openheimer)

A LIFE OF ACTIVISM

You have the right to be involved and something important to contribute. Take the risk.[28]

— Mae Jemison,
White House Conference on STEM

Rhana Bazzini

In Granny D's Footsteps

Marching for social justice

I so envy people who seem to know from an early age what they want to be when they grow up. I was 55 when I finally figured it out: a massage therapist. Of course there were many steps leading up to that discovery.

When asked to contribute to my husband's family history, I described my life as vanilla compared to their rich Italian culture and experiences. And vanilla it was.

I was born on Long Island, New York. Even though I was born in 1933, at the height of the Depression, I was not aware of the devastation that haunted the country. I lived on a lovely quiet street. All the mothers were stay-at-home mothers. There were no girls my age, so my best friends were two boys. We rode our bikes, played hide-and-seek. It was sort of a "Leave it to Beaver" life.

After graduating from a very competitive high school, I wanted a complete change and went to Idaho State College.

It was, indeed, a change. I stayed there for a year and a half, then completed my education at Tufts with a degree in psychology and a minor in education.

A few years went by and I met and fell madly in love with the man I would marry. I must confess it was "lust at first sight." We were fortunate because, even though we were very different, our lust became love. Our lives evolved. In 1958 our only child, a son, was born. We moved from the Bronx to Connecticut, where we had a jewelry store.

The years flew by faster and faster. We retired to Sarasota, Florida, and had a few good years before my spouse started to fail. We had been marred for fifty-six years when he died at home on June 9, 2013. As he said, he'd had a good life and had no regrets.

I've made the journey from daughter to wife to mother to widow. On the racetrack of life, I've felt better with each passing decade. Somehow I felt 80 was going to be a watershed year. On that racetrack at 80, I was rounding the bend with the finish line in sight.

With good health and a lot of time on my hands, I decided to do something to make the world a better place before I crossed that finish line. What I needed was a project. After much thought, Doris "Granny D" Haddock kept popping into my mind. In 1999 at age 89, she started her walk across the country for campaign finance reform. She was a strong force in getting the bipartisan McCain-Feingold Campaign Finance Reform Act passed in 2002. She lived to be 100 and saw it all come apart. I couldn't see her work go for naught, so I decided to reawaken her spirit.

My original plan was to duplicate her walk. I switched to Plan B, recruiting women over 80 to march to their state capitals to support campaign finance reform. I wound up with Plan C, focusing on Florida. It is a step in the right direction.

Rhana Bazzini, 2014
(Photo by Dan Wagner, Herald-Tribune, *May 13, 2014)*

Government dysfunction is not a partisan issue. More than 80% of voters think money plays too big a part in our elections. There has been a huge grassroots effort by a number of organizations and groups working to take back our democracy. We are working toward an amendment to the Constitution that will recognize that money is not speech and that corporations are not people.

When I hear people say that's impossible, I remind them it's happened 27 times.

On my trek to Tallahassee, I will remind people that democracy is not something you have; it's something you do. I will attest that it takes a village. Some wonderful people are working on this mission. If it comes to pass, most of the credit will go to them.

What an adventure it has been already. What inspiring people I've met along the way, and I haven't even started on my trek.

This may just be a pipe dream, but the shame is not in failing but in not trying in the first place. Please wish me luck!

Rhana Bazzini has many more stories to share, about love and joy and family life.

Editor's Note: Rhana completed the 52-day, 430-plus-mile march from Sarasota to Tallahassee on Dec. 3, 2014. Supporters joined her along the way; a crowd of approximately 100 people greeted her arrival.

.

A truly living human being cannot remain neutral.[29]

— NADINE GORDIMER,
quoted by Professor Sture Allén

Sonia Pressman Fuentes

EIGHTY-FIVE YEARS OLD IN SARASOTA COUNTY, FLORIDA

After retirement, the author alters her activist life

At the age of eighty-five, I am experiencing the richest phase of my life. Living in Sarasota County, Florida, I am actively involved as a community and feminist activist, writer, and public speaker. How did that happen and how does it differ from the lives of women my age in the past?

I was born in Berlin, Germany, in 1928 of Polish Jewish parents. In 1933, my brother, who was fourteen years my senior, immediately saw the threat Hitler posed to Germany's Jews and urged my parents to leave. We left that summer, going first to Antwerp, Belgium, and from there to New York City. In 1936, my family moved to the Catskill Mountains, where my father built and ran a summer resort. I graduated as valedictorian of my high school class and went on to Cornell University, from which I graduated Phi Beta Kappa in 1950.

After graduation from Cornell, I could not find a job until I studied shorthand in business school. After that, I worked as a secretary in New York City. By 1954, I felt I was getting nowhere fast, so I began attending the University of Miami School of Law. At that time, about 3 percent of the nation's law school graduates were women. I graduated from law school first in my class in 1957 and moved to Washington, D.C., where I began work as an attorney. I spent the next twenty years with several federal agencies and another ten years as an attorney and executive with two major corporations. The most significant work I did, however, was to co-found NOW (National Organization for Women) and to serve as the first woman attorney in the Office of the General Counsel at the Equal Employment Opportunity Commission. After my retirement in 1993, I did two things that changed my life: I spent 5 1/2 years researching and writing my memoir, *Eat First – You Don't Know What They'll Give You, The Adventures of an Immigrant Family and Their Feminist Daughter*, published in November 1999, and I moved to Sarasota. Since that time, I have been busier than ever. I am constantly being interviewed about my role as a founder of the second wave of feminism and showered with honors.

Several factors led to the life I have led and continue to lead. From the age of ten, I felt that there was a purpose to my life, a mission I had to accomplish, and that I was not free as other girls and women were simply to marry, raise a family, and pursue happiness. Since I had been born only because my mother's favored abortionist was out of Germany, my immediate family and I had escaped the Holocaust, and I was bright, I felt that I had been saved to make a contribution to the world. I found that purpose when I joined the EEOC and began my involvement in the fight for women's rights, which continues to this day.

I began coming to Sarasota County in 1994 as a snowbird and moved here full-time in 2006. Fortunately, I came to a unique community. With a stable population of about 400,000, Sarasota County has the amenities of a much larger place. It is known for its culture and art and has every organization and activity one could imagine. Of course, we don't worry about snow and ice – although our summers are hot and humid and the threat of a hurricane looms over us. However, one needs the financial wherewithal to live here and enjoy what Sarasota has to offer.

Sarasota is nirvana for senior citizens, and I am grateful daily to be living in paradise with a full schedule of social and cultural activities. I work out at the Y, usher for two local theaters, belong to a number of organizations, and have a steady round of lunches, dinners, movies, and theater with friends and organizations.

In the past, senior citizens did not lead the kind of life available in Sarasota today. My image of a senior in the past is of an elderly man or woman sitting in a rocking chair in the back room of an adult child's home waiting to die. That is not the lifestyle of the lucky seniors who have the health and finances to live in Sarasota.

©2014

The Arthur and Elizabeth Schlesinger Library on the History of

Women in America in Cambridge, Massachusetts and the American Jewish Archives in Cincinnati, Ohio have collections of Sonia Pressman Fuentes' papers, CDs, tapes, pictures, and speeches. To learn more about Sonia and her remarkable life, see her website at http://www.erraticimpact.com/fuentes.

Sonia Pressman Fuentes in center with members of Miami Law Women, University of Miami School of Law, 2013

Every moment is an organizing opportunity, every person a potential activist, every minute a chance to change the world.[30]

– DOLORES HUERTA,
"Election Day is the Most Important Day of Your Life"

Helen Isaacson

TAPPING, TEACHING, AND FIDDLING
And, of course, there's politics

I am the oldest – by far – in my tap dance class, 84. One of the greatest pleasures of my mature years is to put on my shiny black shoes and make music with my feet.

When I was four, my mother enrolled me in a ballet class but after three years decided against my continuing. A cousin in the family had become a chorus girl, and this was not what my mother wanted for her only daughter. I was heartbroken; dancing was what made me most happy.

Thirty years ago, when I was still teaching at the University of Michigan and feeling a bit too bound to the desk and to the books and to the papers to grade, I decided I needed to do something physical. Could I possibly return to my childhood love of ballet? One adult ballet class taught me that far too many years had passed since I had been the star of my children's ballet class. Someone suggested I try tap.

Even oldies like me can tap. The great legendary tappers died with their shoes on.

When I moved to Berkeley after retiring, the first thing I looked for was a dance studio; the second was a place where I could do volunteer work. I read that California had begun to spend more money on incarceration than on education, so I volunteered to teach women in a San Francisco jail. I taught in the jail's charter school; I helped in a program for women now separated from their children and started a peer tutoring service so that women who were accomplished in English or math could help those who were not.

Then there are my violin lessons. Many of us grandmothers warn our grandchildren that they will be sorry later if they do not continue playing the piano or violin. Recently I decided to stop simply feeling sorry that I had given up the violin. I had my bow restrung and found a teacher who seems to get a kick out of working with someone my age. Every day (well, almost) I fiddle away to learn anew the right way to place my fingers and hold my wrists. More important, I try to do as my teacher advises – "make my own" the piece I am playing.

And for the sake of my grandchildren, I continue to be active politically in Grandmothers Against War. Every Thursday four or more Grandmothers hand out half-page leaflets explaining a current situation where citizen involvement might make a difference in creating a more peaceful world; we hope that those who take and read our words will use the toll-free telephone numbers we provide to call their congressional representatives and the President.

Everyone knows that being active helps keep you alive. I would die of boredom if I did not have lots to do.

Helen Isaacson was born and brought up in Brooklyn, New York. She met her husband when they were both reporters for the student newspaper at tuition-free Brooklyn College. They married in 1954, lived in Washington, D.C.; London, England; Oberlin, Ohio; Berkeley; Ann Arbor, Michigan; and, finally, again in Berkeley; where they moved after both retired from teaching at the University of Michigan. They have a daughter who lives nearby with her two children and a son who lives in Chicago with his family.

Helen Isaacson at home, 2014
(Photo by Nancy Rubin)

June Brumer

HOW DID I GET HERE FROM BROOKLYN?

A life of educating, organizing, and demonstrating

When I graduated from Brooklyn College at the age of 19 (a big mistake to rush children through school), I was not fit for anything in the labor market. I had majored in political science although I had no idea what that really was. My first job was as a receptionist at the Decca Records recording studio. I got fired because I tried to help organize the office staff into the United Office and Professional Workers union. I had a boyfriend who was entering law school, and I had just read the biography of Clarence Darrow, so I decided that I would become a lawyer. I thought I could help fix things for working people.

Law school was a good choice academically, but I was not ready for a legal career. By the time I had finished at Brooklyn Law School I was married. I passed the New York State Bar, and then my husband and I decided to move to the San Francisco Bay Area. By the time I passed the California Bar, I had two children and had become active in the more progressive branch of the California Democratic Party. I ran for the Oakland School Board but was defeated partly because the Oakland Tribune, then a very right-wing newspaper, wrote that I had been endorsed for office by a so-called red union, the International Longshore and Warehouse Union; – remember Harry Bridges.

In the early 1960s the issue of atomic weapons and testing became part of the public discourse. I received a call from my good friend, Pat Cody, about a new group called Women Strike for Peace. On November 1, 1961, 50,000 women across the U.S. walked out of our kitchens and on to the streets of our cities. In Oakland we marched in front of City Hall, demanding an end to nuclear testing, which was damaging our atmosphere and contaminating the milk that our children were drinking. It was very much a white-gloved, ladylike demonstration. We carried signs such as "No More Strontium 90," "End Nuclear Testing." But that was perhaps the beginning of my more outspoken political activism.

I began to think about ways to encourage more people to understand the political process and what individuals could do to influence it. The run for School Board encouraged me to learn more about the education system in California and in Oakland. I took some education classes at the University of California and decided that part-time teaching would suit my family life better than legal work. I was fortunate to stumble on Oakland Adult Education, which had just begun a day high school for adults. I was hired to teach government and U.S. history for four hours a day. It was a wonderful job. In 1965 the students were serious adults. Later the school attracted many East Oakland residents who were dropouts or throw-outs. Thus, my political activism expressed itself in educating younger people.

Although teachers who taught for 20 hours per week were covered by the collective bargaining contract (California Teachers' Association), my colleagues who worked fewer than 20 hours had no union representation. The rival American Federation of Teachers was willing to organize these teachers, and I worked for it, first as a volunteer, and later as a paid organizer. We succeeded. Adult education part-timers were covered by their own collective bargaining agreement.

After retiring from teaching, I found the Emma Goldman Papers at the University of California, Berkeley. I have been a weekly volunteer there since about 1987, working on the Goldman Papers archive and most recently a four-volume edition of the most important writings of Goldman and her colleagues.

And then, in my 80s, I was introduced to Grandmothers Against the War, a wonderful group that formed because of the wars in Iraq and Afghanistan. My job has been to organize visits to local high schools by military veterans. They give young people information about military life that the military recruiters, who are on every campus in working-class communities in our area, don't provide.

I guess that my life today is just a continuation of what I've always done, although my energy is much more limited. I'm considering other activities, such as literacy training with adults, that will satisfy my need to improve what I believe needs improving in our country. But then again, maybe I'll find the time to read the books that have been piling up for the past 10 years!

June Brumer's activism was truly enabled by her husband, Abe, who declared, "Some women like to hang out in bars. My wife likes to organize, educate, and demonstrate; what can I do?" According to June, he was a good man who died about 12 years ago. They had two daughters who, with their husbands, are kind and good people who understand and fulfill their responsibilities to their families and the larger community and have imparted this attitude to their children. June believes she's had a very lucky and fulfilled life.

June Brumer, Oakland, California, 1978

I know you got to disturb the peace
when you can't get no peace.[31]

— ARETHA FRANKLIN,
offering to post bail for Angela Davis in the 1970s

Leita Kaldi Davis

NOT YOUR MOTHER'S CUP OF TEA

A life of adventure, capped by a marriage at 70

How did a nice girl like me from a small town in upstate New York end up in Paris, Rome, Budapest, in a bush village in Africa, and in the hinterlands of Haiti? I must have been born with the wanderlust gene and a wayward sense of reality, though my mother warned that I was a dreamer.

After spending eight years in Europe, then raising an Italian son and a Hungarian son in the States, I escaped once they were grown to become a Peace Corps volunteer in Senegal, West Africa at age 55. Three years of bliss in a remote bush village where the Sahara meets the Atlantic, living without electricity or plumbing, among the most beautiful people I've ever known. They taught me concepts of Islam and animism. Though I thought that my efforts to help the Sérère people were often fraught with misunderstandings and mishap, I was able, in the end, to touch the lives of many of them. There was the boy, Bayalou, whom I saved from being a cripple; Coulibali, whose butik business improved with my retailing tips; Omar, the artiste autodidact, who went from drawing in the sand to becoming a successful painter; women's groups, with whom I worked to improve their businesses, building warehouses for their shellfish and millet, or selling handcrafted artifacts to tourists. I learned wisdom, forgiveness and goodness from these greatest teachers of the planet, the poor.

After three years in Senegal, I got a job in Haiti as administrator of Hospital Albert Schweitzer, where I stayed for five years. Initially filled with the purest intentions, I lost my innocence when confronted with *revolutionnaires* and *vagabons* who threatened my life and the existence of the hospital and its community development programs. By comparison, *voudou* was fun. I also had many tender experiences in my daily life, inspired by Haitians with whom I worked – the doctors, nurses, agronomists, my housemaid, and many others who taught me surprising lessons in dignity, faith and forgiveness. My son's visits

Leita Kaldi Davis in Florida, 2014

were joyful respites, and his marriage to an elite Haitian woman provided a keyhole through which I observed the dynamics of class and
prejudice among the layers of Haitian society. Most important was my
relationship with Gwen Grant Mellon, who co-founded the hospital in
1956 with her husband, Dr. Larimer Mellon of the Pittsburgh Mellons.
They spent their lives serving people in the Artibonite Valley.

After I retired, I married at the age of 70 – my greatest adventure!
I'd always felt that a relationship would be life's most frightening
challenge, but my loving husband made it easy. Plus he likes travel
adventures too, and we go bar hopping and swing dancing a lot. Not
what I'd call my mother's cup of tea.

Leita Kaldi Davis is the author of Roller Skating in the Desert
(Senegal) and In the Valley of Atibon *(Haiti) available on amazon.
com or from lkaldi@hotmail.com. In other lifetimes, she worked at
the United Nations in New York, UNESCO in Paris, at the Fletcher
School of Law and Diplomacy, and Harvard University. She suppos-
edly retired in Florida in 2002.*

Vicki Ryder

"You're Never Too Old To Raise a Little Hell"

Arrested in North Carolina

"You're never too old to raise a little hell!" So said "Granny D" (Doris Haddock) who, at the age of 89, walked clear across America to call attention to the need for campaign finance reform and the dangers of mixing money and politics.

And so it was that, at the age of 71 and inspired by Granny D's message, I found myself being handcuffed and carted off to jail.

It all started when my husband and I retired and moved to North Carolina in 2011. Soon after we settled into our home-to-be, we began to hear about laws being enacted in our new home state that would deny Medicaid expansion funds to half a million of our citizens, cut folks off from their unemployment benefits, make it harder for many to vote, allow fracking and other dangerous environmental practices to poison our waters, and force 15 of our 16 women's reproductive health centers to close.

While watching the news on a Monday late in April 2013, I heard that 17 people had been arrested at the State Legislature while mounting a peaceful protest against these regressive laws. I knew that my retirement years were supposed to be spent visiting grandchildren, knitting sweaters, and baking bread, but I just couldn't just sit back and watch when so many other grandmothers (and grandchildren) would be so callously affected.

I remembered my own grandmother, who had taught me the words of the great Rabbi Hillel:

> *"If I am not for myself, who will be for me?*
> *But if I am only for myself, then what am I?*
> *And if not now, when?"*

And so, the following Monday, I joined the protests that came to be known as Moral Mondays. Along with 30 others, I entered the Legislative Building, where we sang and chanted and prayed for more humane and just laws that would meet the needs of our citizens. And, when the police chief ordered us to leave, I chose to stand firm.

My mind was clear and filled with memories: of my mother's participation in the struggle for a woman's right to vote… of my father's fight for more humane working conditions… of myself at the Lincoln Memorial in 1963 when I heard Martin Luther King Jr. deliver his "I have a dream" speech… of friends who could not get help when they found themselves alone and pregnant…

My mind was filled with current visions, too: of veterans and other homeless people begging in the streets… of teacher layoffs and public school closings and toxic spills… of my friend Kathy as she wept when her daughter died because she was denied health insurance coverage…

It was all too much. If I had learned anything in my 71 years it was that if change was needed, then I needed to act. Democracy, I had been taught, was not a spectator sport.

After 13 weeks of Moral Monday protests, a total of 941 North Carolinians had put their bodies on the line and gone to jail for justice. Their trials continue to this day. In the meantime, more and more people have joined our Moral Monday movement, which is now spreading throughout the nation. And, when the North Carolina Legislature comes back into session, I'll be there again… raising a little hell!

Vicki Ryder had varied careers as teacher, public relations coordinator, and mediator before retiring in 2004. A social activist all her life, she is a member of the Raging Grannies and writes many of the lyrics for the songs they sing, giving voice to their protests against war, economic and social injustice, and the corporate rape of the environment. The grandmother of three, Vicki now lives in Durham, North Carolina, with her husband and their dog.

Vicki Ryder in hat and mug shot, Raleigh, North Carolina, 2013

THE IMPACT OF FEMINISM

*You're not allowed to retire from women's issues because
someone's going to pull the rug out from under you.* [32]
— Virginia Whitehill,
She's Beautiful When She's Angry

Rose Glickman

MY LIFE AS A MODERN WOMAN

A life shaped by Marxism and feminism

Be forewarned: This is a feminist story, shaped by the confluence of Jewish Marxist immigrant parents and the flowering of the women's movement in the 1960s. My parents took seriously the Marxist version of female emancipation – perhaps more seriously than Marx and his followers intended. Their daughter would be educated and have a profession. It was never even discussed in our household, it was simply accepted. That made me a proto-feminist. What I mean by that is that I grew up with their convictions but uncomfortable, occasionally miserable, with the larger culture's dicta about what I didn't have the right to expect. I had no vocabulary, no one to talk to, just a kind of crude road map to guide me on rather mysterious terrain. In my graduate school class of 350 students at the University of Chicago in the late '50s and early '60s, I was one of three women. Never in my entire university career did I have a woman professor. Working on my doctoral dissertation, divorced and raising a baby on my own, a single woman striving for a career in a boys' club: a dime a dozen today, not so then. Just at the right moment the Women's Movement burst forth and gave me the gift of a vocabulary, an explanation of what was wrong with the world and why, comrades, community and hope.

As I write this, my age is 3 to the 4th power. Figure it out. In my mother's generation that would have been very old. And it is old. But a different "old" to the eons of our forebears.

I have had three full careers. For twenty-five years I taught Russian history, European history, and finally women's history. I was among very few scholars privileged to spend a lot of time doing research in the Soviet Union during Cold War years and subsequently (in fact, to this day). I wrote one of the first books in the world on the history of Russian women, a few articles, and I loved it all: teaching, research, writing. But I was still in the boys' club and never entirely comfortable, although I had many close friends in the academic community. My academic career was mainly in the San Francisco Bay Area because I could not bring myself to take a job, no matter how good, in an unappealing place. Twenty-five years later my luck as a freelance academic without a stable affiliation ran out: too advanced for many jobs (What! Take you on as an assistant professor at your age?) and too few publications to compete at the top. At this point, I'm in my fifties. In this brave new world I was ready for another adventure. I also wanted to do another kind of writing. So I left academia, wrote a book called *Daughters of Feminists* about the daughters of my generation of feminists in the USA.

Writing that book was not going to put food on the table. Who would take on a woman of my age in or out of academia? Cashing in on my fluent Russian, I took a job resettling the Soviet Jews who were now allowed to emigrate and did so in great numbers to the USA. In other words, I became a social worker in a new world of different experiences, developing skills I never dreamed I had and finding new rewards. Then the Russians stopped coming.

Approaching 70, I again used my knowledge of Russia and fluency in the language to work with an extraordinary medical nonprofit that goes to Russia to teach Russian doctors how to care for babies that would otherwise die. Again, a new, complex, and amazing world. I have done that for 12 years. I'm not sure what is next, but I am sure that there is a "next."

Marx's well-intentioned formulation of women's emancipation was necessary but not sufficient. Education, work, independence – not to be sneezed at, as my parents would have said. To the women's movement, Feminism, I owe as much, probably more: validation of my struggle for a wonderful work life and in every other facet of my life, knowledge, words, courage to defy other conventions, to have the life my mother could only have dreamed of. I rejoice in what young women can do today, wish I had had so much of what they have, and despair at what remains to be done, all over the world.

Rose Glickman's first book, Russian Factory Women: Workplace and Society, 1880-1914, *was published in 1984. She has translated a historical biography,* Agnessa: From Paradise to Purgatory, A Voice from Stalin's Russia, *published in 2012. Rose has one daughter and two grandkids who, alas, live in France.*

Rose Glickman at home, 2014
(Photo by Nancy Rubin)

I raise up my voice – not so I can shout but so that those without a voice can be heard... We cannot all succeed when half of us are held back. [33]

– MALALA YOUSAFZAI,
"Malala Yousafzai speech in full"

Evelyn Torton Beck

NEVER IN MY WILDEST DREAMS

Sacred Circle Dance transforms the author's feminist path

Evelyn Torton Beck leading the dance at Ghost Ranch, 2011

Never in my wildest dreams did I imagine that I would be teaching Sacred Circle Dance at age 81. As a child, I did not have the luxury of imagining my life forward. Often it seemed as if I were making my life up, only to discover that I was following a multi-stranded thread: teaching, social justice, and dancing.

From the beginning, I loved school. But because of Hitler's anti-Semitism in Austria (where I was born), I was evicted from kindergarten. We escaped to Italy and in first grade I earned a gold star. When I was 7, we immigrated to the USA, and from the beginning, school was my haven. Home was chaos and anguish over the fate of close relatives.

From early on, I also loved to teach. In high school I was chosen to be "teacher for a day" though I was not the best student – likely the most enthusiastic. Living at home while attending college, I had no idea of what I was capable. PTSD and a noisy household distracted me, but with the help of worldly friends, I got into graduate school to study teaching.

Although I suspected I was lesbian in my teens, the idea was so frightening in those years that coming out seemed impossible. Like so many other hidden lesbians, I married and had two children. Against peer pressure, I returned to school where I became a teaching assistant. After 10 years, I earned a PhD in literature and eventually became a professor. In time, I became a founder of women's studies, lesbian studies, and Jewish women's studies. When feminism made the word lesbian speakable, I came out, and thrived.

The realization that many women's studies students had histories of trauma led me to train as a therapist, a different kind of teacher, and after 13 years, I earned a PhD in clinical psychology.

I came upon Sacred Circle Dance seemingly by chance, but from the first step, I felt I had come home; it was like the folk dancing of my youth but more nourishing. The "sacred" in our dance is not religious but is related to wholeness and healing. The dances are moving meditations integrating mind, body and spirit, leading to harmony and balance.

I danced weekly but soon went for longer trainings. I became so passionate that when one of our local teachers decided not to teach, I stepped in and never again stepped out.

Sacred Circle Dance changed my path from feminist professor to feminist therapist to feminist teacher of dance. To support this practice, I use all my previous trainings. In the early years of feminism, there had been a sharp split between spirituality and politics, though some had tried to integrate the two. At that time you could not be both, and I chose politics.

But by the time I started to teach dance, I was in my late sixties and no longer accepted false divisions, no longer worried about losing my feminist credentials. In this stage of my life, I would be my most authentic self.

I began to learn anew and organized dance sessions celebrating goddesses around the world, honoring the muses of creativity, the seasons and stages of women's lives, opening to joy, healing, wisdom, gratitude, world peace, and being fully present in our bodies. The dance has become a central part of my spiritual practice.

I no longer see a separation between trying to change the world and focusing on individual and communal strengths. Our dance practice builds community and offers a safe haven.

One culmination of this practice is a weeklong workshop at Ghost Ranch, where Georgia O'Keeffe painted; in 2014, a Celebration of Crones in Autumn.

Although I had a lobe of my lung removed three years ago and last year had a bout of lower back pain, miraculously this never interfered with my ability to dance. I am fortunate to be able to move freely and joyfully. I forget that others may see me as old. I intend to keep on teaching so long as I can dance. My passion for teaching these dances is so strong that I think it is contagious.

Among the research interests of Evelyn (Evi) Torton Beck, Professor Emerita, Women's Studies, University of Maryland is the healing power of art (in the life and work of Kahlo and Kafka) and of dance in the lives of older women. She is the author of Kafka and the Yiddish Theater *and* Nice Jewish Girls: A Lesbian Anthology. *She offers Sacred Circle dance classes and workshops (in the Washington, D.C. area), at professional meetings, and at Ghost Ranch in New Mexico. See the websites: www.evibeck.com and www.sacredcircle-dancedc.com.*

Evelyn Torton Beck, 2008

Kathyrn K. Johnson

MAKING GENDER TROUBLE

The Women's Movement influences the author's life

A white binder bearing the title *Third Stage* sits on my desk. An image of blue sky and green grass graces its cover. In this binder, I keep newspaper clippings, notes and articles about all the things I intend to do before I die. Next to my computer is a note card with words written by George Elliot: *It is never too late to be what you might have been.* Elliot, famous author, journalist, and poet *ne'* Mary Ann Evans, assumed this pen name to be taken seriously as a writer. She ought to know.

The late Rosemary Park, then president of Barnard College, got me started on my life's trajectory. At the fall college-wide junior year convocation in 1965, President Park challenged the assembled young women: *Why does Barnard have you in an all-women's college at a time when you are biologically ready to mate? Her answer: You are here across from the all-male Columbia University to gain knowledge without distraction so that before you are married, after you raise your children, and in the 12 years you are on your own as a widow you will have something to think and talk about.*

If Rosemary Park fueled my dissatisfaction with the limits of women's role, then sociology professor Renée Fox fired my imagination and nurtured my commitment to higher education and sociology. Despite my mother's dire warning that *no man would marry me if I got a PhD,* I went to the University of California, Berkeley for graduate school in sociology. After one year, I dutifully married a fellow sociology graduate student. Caught up in the cauldron of '60s Berkeley politics, I left graduate school with my master's degree and the parting words to my soon-to-be ex-husband, *You can study social change, I will make it!*

I found my home in the women's movement and made my career in higher education in applied sociology as a policy analyst, research associate, and coordinator for special projects at the University of

California on the Berkeley and Davis campuses, the UC Office of the President, the Wright Institute, Berkeley and San Francisco State University. My work has centered on creating interdisciplinary-based programs to make undergraduate education relevant to students' lives, to promoting gender and multicultural equity and to making the university responsible to the community of which it is a part.

Whenever possible, I have used my university position to raise awareness about women's issues, to promote feminist scholarship, to increase educational opportunities for women faculty and students and to fight for public education as a member of the Vampire Slayers agitprop collective. Off campus, my politics haven't changed, but my activism has shifted from street demonstrations to electoral politics and international women's issues.

Ten years ago, I decided it wasn't enough to create programs. Other Second Wave feminists more famous than I write memoirs. My choice: to finish my graduate studies (orals, 1981) and write my dissertation, despite the fact that my sister-in-law said it wasn't *age-appropriate*.

My decision was two-fold: I wanted my own voice. I wanted to contribute to the women's community that has defined and enriched my adult life. The dissertation is titled: *Making Gender Trouble and Telling our Stories: The Fate of Feminist Idealism and Oppositional Gender Practices Among SF/Bay Area 2nd Wave Feminists:1967-'75.*

Although I could, I have not retired. When I do, my goal is to write angry but articulate op-ed pieces on women's issues and become a consultant to an international women's human rights organization. For my birthday, my son gave me a safari jacket.

In her university positions as an advocate for women, Kathyrn K. Johnson taught the first women's health course at UC Berkeley, wrote a report titled Academic Barriers for UC Davis Women Faculty and, at San Francisco State University, established a Stay in School CAL Works Family Resource Center, a program on gender and public policy, an annual SFSU Women's History Month lecture series, and a SFSU interdisciplinary feminist seminar. Off campus she was a co-founder of the San Francisco Democratic Women in Action, and a SF Commission and Department on the Status of Women's delegate to the

Annual United Nations Women's Conference.

Kathyrn K. Johnson in her safari jacket, 2014

Yet if a woman never lets herself go, how will she ever know
how far she might have got? If she never takes off her high-
heeled shoes, how will she ever know how far she could walk,
or how fast she could run?[34]

— GERMAINE GREER,
The Change: Women, Aging and the Menopause

Gloria J. Sandoval

WHEN DOMESTIC VIOLENCE WAS SILENCED

(ORIGINALLY TITLED NOT YOUR GRANDMOTHER'S FEMINISM)

The author, once an abused feminist, moves on

I am a 62-year-old woman living in the San Francisco Bay Area. I grew up in American Canyon and attended Catholic schools. I was always very close to my mother and grandmother. Their strength of character made them role models for me.

My father used to say I was born a feminist. I remember being fairly young and declaring that I wanted to be the first woman president. My mom and dad told me I could do anything I set my mind to. I believed it.

In high school, I was into politics. I was on the student council every year, was an editor for the teen page of the newspaper, sat on the leadership team of the Robert F. Kennedy Young Democrats and walked precincts and had doors slammed in my face many times, mostly when advocating for gun control.

My college years were a whirlwind. Keeping up my grades at UC Berkeley wasn't easy. I worked; my parents didn't have the means to pay tuition. I took more units than required and went to school in the summer because I wanted to graduate in three years and save money. Then there were the hippies and the anti-war protests. Berkeley gave me the opportunity to participate in both, and I did. Tear-gassed on several occasions, I somehow managed to avoid being arrested.

And I was in love. Rick and I grew up as neighbors: he the neighborhood "hoodlum," I the "goody two shoes." But I saw his potential. I told everyone who was concerned (including my parents) that deep down, Rick was a really nice guy, bruised by hard knocks. With a girlfriend like me, I said, he would surely change for the better.

Our relationship was always abusive. During our courtship it was verbal and emotional abuse. He called me names, taunted me about working so hard and controlled who my friends were and how I spent my time. Although these should have been big red flags for me, they weren't. I chalked up his behavior to how much he loved me. After all, in those days, domestic violence was silenced; it was still a hidden family issue.

I married Rick the summer after graduation. Although I had been admitted to U.C. Berkeley School of Law, I decided to take a year off to work.

In my job as a counselor for a diversion program, I worked with many attorneys and decided law school wasn't for me. I figured I was such a bleeding heart I would probably spend years (and lots of money) in school and turn out to be a poor public defender. Besides, I really enjoyed the social work aspect of my job.

During those years the abuse increased and became physical as well. Rick would threaten my life if I ever talked about ending the relationship. And I was pregnant.

After our son was born, I found a new job at a rape crisis center, working part-time so I could spend more time with my baby. The center was a small fledgling nonprofit with only three part-time employees. Within a year, our executive director was recruited to another agency and the board of directors hired me to replace her.

So here I was, the executive director of a feminist rape crisis center, spending my days talking about violence against women and children and going home to an abusive partner. It became clear that either my marriage or my profession had to change.

I decided to leave my relationship. My son was four years old. I had left many times previously, only to be found or be convinced that it would never happen again. I was the typical battered woman.

My work to end violence against women and children intensified, and I stayed at the rape crisis center for 15 years. I then spent 5 years as executive director of Shanti, which provides volunteer-based emotional and practical support for people living with life-threatening or chronic illnesses. For the last 17 years, I have been CEO of an agency dedicated to ending family violence.

My adult son is a wonderful, feminist man, married to a strong and beautiful woman, and they have blessed me with an incredible granddaughter who is the love of my life.

I often think about how different my life is from my grandmother's, how many opportunities I had that she and my mother didn't. Even so, I am struck by how their strength of character, their determination and their feminism were instilled in me.

Someday, I hope my granddaughter will say the same about me.

When she is not working her "day" job, Gloria Sandoval enjoys consulting on organizational development, spending time with her granddaughter, reading, and camping with family.

Gloria Sandoval in her office, 2012

THE LONGER VIEW

We older women who know we aren't heroines can offer
our younger sisters, at the very least, an honest report
of what we have learned and how we have grown.[35]

— ELIZABETH JANEWAY,
"Breaking the Age Barrier"

Rochelle Gatlin

FROM DR. ROCHELLE GATLIN TO DH MEDHAHSHRI

Late in life, the author becomes a Buddhist

Hauling the contents of four large file drawers to the recycling bin recently, I threw out 43 years of my life, years spent teaching at various colleges. The latest, and the only full-time tenured position I held, was as a history instructor at City College of San Francisco. I loved teaching and creating innovative courses at San Francisco State University, California State University Sacramento, and City College of San Francisco, but I did not publish enough or develop a disciplinary specialty, so from the academic viewpoint I was not a success.

Although I was taking a financial risk, I retired in 2011 at age 68. My love of teaching was being eroded by changes in education to which I was not adapting well, from new technology to the growing focus on "outcomes." I was becoming exhausted because I had to take public transportation, teach night courses, and endure a chilly wind (if not worse) after class. I was developing peripheral artery disease, which made it difficult to walk quickly. I never got enough sleep. It was no surprise that I loved my students less and was becoming irritated with them. I needed to leave for their sake and mine.

Fortunately, I had managed not to get pregnant in high school (unlike some of my friends) and my boyfriend broke up with me instead of marrying me. That heartbreak and the label of bad girl (no longer a virgin) had inspired me to leave home for college. It was a smart decision, probably the best I made until 2005, when I walked into the San Francisco Buddhist Center.

I was coming up for a sabbatical. I noticed a sign, "Drop-in Meditation," and thought "Well, that can't hurt." Maybe it would calm me, keep me from waking up angry every day. It was a yellow building on a small street, with a meditation space (shrine room) that had been beautifully stripped down to brick walls with a polished wood floor and a big red Buddha. I decided not to start buying and reading the tempting books on the shelves because I knew it would be all too easy to make Buddhism just another intellectual pursuit. I wanted to see if meditation did anything for me. What I liked was sitting and doing nothing for ever longer periods; that seemed radical and even a gift to myself. One of the practices, *metta bhavana* or loving-kindness, was making a difference. My heart seemed to become softer instead of feeling like a stone. I had thought that one was either a kind and generous person or one was not. I had not really believed that at my age, I could change. Well, change or impermanence is at the heart of Buddhism; therefore, kindness and compassion and other good (or what Buddhists call "skillful") qualities and habits can be developed, and "unskillful" emotional and mental habits can be lessened, even eradicated.

Once I started to study the *dharma* (the Buddha's teachings), this made sense, and it had enough psychological sophistication to satisfy my intellectual snobbery. It took me longer to participate in the devotional aspects of Buddhism, not just meditation and study but also devotion, ritual, and an openness to the mythic, the mystical, the transcendent. It reminded me of what I had found appealing in the 1960s counterculture but without the drugs and with far more structure and purpose.

I approached the *sangha* with skepticism. Fearing a cult, I had to run its members through my intellectual and political tests. Certainly not all are intellectuals or love books, but they are intelligent, sometimes irreverent and often artistically creative. Even better, I began to appreciate kindness in people more than quick, sharp wit. What I especially admire is their hard-won joy, which comes not by denying suffering and death but by facing them and sharing these experiences truthfully and fully.

Sometimes I can hardly believe what has happened. Religion was not part of my life plan. Formally joining a religious community, taking vows, and being given a new name, Medhahshri, impossible. Now, I am not a monk or nun, not a priest or priestess, but not quite a lay person either. I am a *Dharmacharini* (Dh), a *dharmafarer*, or follower of the *dharma*. I don't wear robes but do wear a *kasa* (a kind of cloth collar) for events at the Buddhist Center.

I am growing older, less agile, with a decline in vision and physical energy, but I am happier than ever. My dearest friend died seven years ago, but I am part of a loving and supportive community that includes practical help when someone is ill, recovering from an accident or surgery, or even in financial distress. My ordination at a retreat in New Hampshire included a solemn and meaningful taking of vows but also so much delight, affection, rejoicing, and laughter that it felt like the wedding I never had and the senior prom I never attended.

The daughter of Jewish immigrants who didn't finish high school but shared a deep love of learning, Rochelle Gatlin earned a PhD and became a college professor and an author. Only after she retired did she find the fulfillment she had never imagined in her life.

Rochelle Gatlin, wearing her *kasa* at her ordination, New Hampshire, 2017

Hilde Hein

I WAS ONE OF THE LUCKY ONES

A long productive life after escaping Nazism

I was one of the lucky ones. Even without the menace of Nazism, I would not have fared as well growing up in a middle-class Jewish family in Germany. And, had we stayed, as planned, in 1930s New York, I might have gone to Ethical Culture Fieldston School and absorbed the upper-class American formation, but circumstances drove us westward to what was then the backwater of California, best known for its missions, pottery, porches and sundresses. Shortly after arriving there, my brother and I took part in a celebration of statehood – he as a cowboy and I as a cow. We were strangers in that environment not only as Jews but as immigrants – perhaps not welcome ones as our leaked FBI files and our unusually long wait to achieve citizenship revealed.

The war years brought radical shifts with the influx of shipyards, Japanese exclusion, and submarine scares. My father, an obstetrician, became a draft medical examiner. I made a MacArthur scrapbook in junior high school and visited the world's fair on Treasure Island. I was a Brownie and briefly a Girl Scout – but not a successful seller of cookies. My friends in high school were a motley mix of class and religion. We swam in the Berkeley Women's City Club pool, bought doughnuts on Telegraph Avenue, and I got my first real job (after babysitting) at Éclair Pastries Bakery, where I folded boxes, put cookies on trays, and eventually graduated to salesgirl status.

Through the left-wing circles of my parents' friends I learned of Reed College and studied there for two years. But observing that everyone was too much like me, I sought more options and moved eastward to complete my bachelor's degree at Cornell. Having discovered philosophy as a distribution requirement, I majored in the subject and have never regretted that choice. I also met my future husband in a German literature class. After my post-graduate year in France, we married and went on to graduate school in Michigan, where I gave birth to three children and a PhD – the latter completed in Pasadena, where my husband did a post-doctoral gig at Cal Tech.

Returning to the east coast, we settled in Newton, Massachusetts, renowned for its good schools, and both of us became academics. I loved ideas and soon came to love the students as well. I think the 1960s are badly misrepresented; for me it was a time of political and intellectual ferment like no other. Civil rights, the anti-Vietnam War movement and emerging feminism were commitments that absorbed the entire family – perhaps, in the end, disrupted it. I taught in a Catholic college, where I was tolerated, tenured, but not promoted. Still – it enabled me to study, teach and publish without interference and to create fast friendships.

When President Kennedy introduced the Peace Corps, I was inspired but unable to abandon my family, so I waited until retirement. I joined at 68 and celebrated my 70th birthday in Morocco, where I taught English at a university midway between Casablanca and Marrakech. I made good friends there and introduced a number of visiting Americans to Morocco. In addition to teaching, I found work in the sole Jewish museum in an Arab country, where, albeit Jews have a long historical presence, few of them remain. This complicated exposure was possibly the most transformative of my Peace Corps adventures. It involved me in every aspect of running a museum, from labeling objects to writing promotional materials and escorting school groups and visiting dignitaries. It also caused me, in still another context, to reflect upon my own Jewishness.

I was in Rabat when 9/11 occurred. While panic struck the U.S., I was safe and warmly cared for in a Muslim country. Undoubtedly Islamist extremism intensified but, upon returning, I found my own country profoundly altered – introverted and mistrustful.

No longer regularly employed, I was fortunate to become affiliated with the Brandeis University Women's Studies Research Center, where I continue my research on museums and public art and combine this with feminist theory. Like most institutions, museums have been radically infused with new technologies and multicultural exposure. Women have long figured as a presence there, but feminist ideas have not. My objective is to put theory to work affecting change in an actual

Hilde with Exploratorium staff at celebration of what would have been
Exploratorium founder Frank Oppenheimer's (Hilde's cousin)
104th birthday, San Francisco, California, 2016
(Photo from www.exploratorium.edu/blogs/spectrum)

Hilde Hein, Massachusetts, 2014

institution. The goal is not to achieve equality in a world that men have constructed (badly) but to use theory beneficently to redesign the world.

June 4, 2014

Hilde Hein recently published Museums and Public Art: A Feminist Vision. *Earlier books include* The Exploratorium: The Museum as Laboratory *(1990),* The Museum in Transition *(2000), and* Public Art: Thinking Museums Differently *(2006). A professor of philosophy at Holy Cross College (1970-2000), she also taught at Los Angeles State College, Tufts University, and Boston University. She resides in Newton, Massachusetts.*

You don't choose the day you enter the world and you don't choose the day you leave. It's what you do in between that makes all the difference.[36]

— ANITA SEPTIMUS,
"The Ultimate List of Inspirational Travel Quotes"

Bella Comelo

LITTLE OLD LADIES SHOULDN'T DO THIS

Forget sitting on the sidelines

I grew up in Mumbai, India. Though it is a cosmopolitan city, there were always restrictions on what girls could do. Arranged marriages were still the norm in the 1950s.

Parents and the community frowned upon dating. When I worked, I had to be careful not to get friendly with young men who were not acceptable to my parents. At age 24, I had an arranged marriage. The good thing was that my parents were a bit liberal; they left the final choice to me. Fortunately, my husband was liberal too and encouraged me to go to graduate school.

Within a few years, we were blessed with four beautiful children. We worked hard to provide a good home for them and migrated to the United States in 1983.

At work I was drawn, by fluke, into the labor movement. I felt the need to be active as I observed that workers, especially immigrants, were exploited in certain areas. I joined the union and held many important positions. I joined picket lines and chanted *"Si se puede"* and "No justice, no peace." My friends from back home would have been shocked to see me. I was involved officially in the union for about 15 years. I was one of the founding members of the Asian Pacific American Labor Alliance, which today has chapters in many U.S. cities. As a national board member, I attended many leadership conferences and workshops and, at age 76, I still participate in picket lines and rallies.

Battling worker exploitation and pursuing the cause of social justice have become dear to me. I have worked on getting living wage ordinances passed in many cities in the San Francisco Bay Area, especially in San Leandro. I am also on the committee of the Faith Alliance for Moral Economy in the Bay Area, which permits me to remain involved in social justice activities.

As they say, one thing leads to another. For the last 12 years, I have served on the Ethnic Pastoral Council of the Oakland Diocese. This council was formed to make sure that all ethnic Catholics were welcomed and to make sure that all ethnic groups assimilate well in the church. Almost every year the council sponsors an ethnic festival called Chautauqua at which ethnic groups come together to share their cultures and forms of worship. At this festival, which honors St. Mary, the liturgy is conducted in Spanish, Tagalog, Hindi, Kumuu, Portuguese, Fijian, Korean, Polish and other languages.

In 2007, I learned that I have kidney disease. This unnerved me a bit, so I started working on my bucket list. I had always wanted to publish a children's book, so I hurried to publish my first, "Raju and the Snake Charmer," which is dedicated to my first grandchild, Milan Ferus Comelo.

One thing that keeps me going and gives me zest for life is my love for my family and my grandkids. A friend thinks I should de-clutter my house, throw out the old photos and live a serene homebound life since I am old and have health issues.

No. My books and the old photos and artifacts from my travels give me comfort and pleasure. So, old folks like me, keep doing whatever makes you happy and comfortable. Forget about negative folks. Would some of my friends or my mom do some of the things I do at 76? I doubt it.

Since 2008, I have served on the Commission of Aging in San Leandro. In this capacity, I encourage our seniors to attend the senior center and take care of their bodies and minds. The city presented me with a leadership award in 2013. Though it is good to be recognized, my involvement in causes has given me more pleasure and happiness than I can express. I feel fulfilled. I can say with some confidence what Little Old Ladies shouldn't do: Do not sit on your butts; keep moving.

Bella Comelo, who holds bachelor of education and master of arts degrees, lives in San Leandro, California with her husband of 52 years, Ernest. She has written for several publications, including Eve's Weekly *in Bombay,* Catholic Voice, India West *newspaper,* Goanet-Femnet *and the* San Leandro Times. *Her new hobby is learning to grow organic vegetables.*

Bella Comelo at home, 2016

It's never too late – in fiction or life – to revise.[37]

– NANCY THAYER,
Morning

Lydia Gans

On Reaching Seniorhood

The author's life changed – so did her wardrobe

Old age doesn't mean what it used to. We're living far longer than our grandmothers' generation, years beyond raising children and even grandchildren. What are we doing with all those extra years? We have opportunities to make new associations, to learn new and different skills, to play a different role in our communities. I'm living that to the fullest.

The changes in my wardrobe are as a good as anything to define the metamorphoses of my role in the world. In my 30 years as a college professor it was skirts and blouses, nylons, heels (though thanks to the women's movement, slacks became acceptable). When I embarked on a new career as a freelance journalist name brand T-shirts and comfortable shoes became my wardrobe. Now I'm an activist for peace and social justice and wear jeans from thrift stores and T-shirts with political messages printed on them.

I taught in the California State University system at Cal Poly Pomona. I loved teaching – and my students liked me. I even managed to get them to like statistics when we got into subjects like the phoniness in public opinion polls and drug company advertising. When I started, I was one of only two women in the mathematics department. Sexism was rampant. It took years of activism to get promoted. I ran for office and was elected president of the faculty union and subsequently to the Academic Senate. I learned to speak out, I learned to advocate.

Once my kids left for college, the world became my home. Summers, sabbatical leaves, and I was out of the country. Lecturing, researching, volunteering, exploring. I renewed a teenage passion for photography and eventually produced a considerable portfolio of photographs and mounted several shows. Photography led to a new career.

My aging father in Berkeley drew me to the Bay Area. Retiring from the university system at 57 wasn't the wisest economic decision but I don't want for anything.

I took an inspiring photojournalism class at San Francisco State. I

Lydia Gans at home, 2015
(Photo by Nancy Rubin)

enrolled at Studio One Art Center in Oakland to learn darkroom techniques and soon, with my sons' help, converted a laundry room into a darkroom. I became a freelance photojournalist. Magazines, newspapers, agencies sent me out to take pictures for their stories. I loved the life. And I relished the evenings spent in the darkroom, watching images I had photographed during the day appear like magic in the developing solution.

It didn't last. Digital cameras came on the scene. Many reporters now take their own pictures. I write the articles to go with the photos. I'm out in the streets talking with people who are homeless, who have physical and mental health issues, who need help that is not there for them. I write about issues like lack of affordable housing and homeless shelters or grossly understaffed mental health facilities, in an effort to stimulate community interest and action.

I nourish my soul singing with Berkeley Community Chorus, my mind volunteering at Chabot Observatory, my need for action with Food Not Bombs.

Lydia Gans was born in Berlin, Germany, in 1931. Her parents were fortunate to find a sponsor who made it possible to get visas and emigrate to America. They arrived in New York in January 1938, a month before Lydia's seventh birthday. Lydia grew up in Manhattan, went to Hunter High School, graduated at 17 and took the train to Berkeley.

Kaye Sykes Williams

MY MOTHER

A tribute to the author's 77-year-old mother

The Ridge is a rural community located in Covington County Mississippi. The residents are all Negroes and most can trace their lineage back to when the slaves were released after the Civil War. They tend to carefully follow the pattern of their ancestors as their example of how to live a fulfilling life. Families are unadorned and minimalists, their intention is to live an honest and clean life, working their modest farms.

During the early 1900s there were several families that had the courage to live a life of hope. They envisioned a time and place in America where they could obtain an education, participate in the political process and gain employment on a level where they could support their families and also have job satisfaction. A common thread among these families was unwavering faith in the Lord that he would see them through their present state and would bless their children. So, with each baby born, parents would privately select the family they hoped their children would marry into when they came of age. This practice perpetuated innocence and folksiness among the residents in the community. Heirs to a few acres of land, this is how life was for my mother's family on The Ridge.

My mother, Laura Dean Lucas Sykes, was born on The Ridge in 1937. She married my father, Q.V. Sykes, when she was just 19 years old. They had three children in the first five years of their marriage and eventually moved to Meridian, Mississippi. Mama's joy was caring for us and supporting my father as he worked as a teacher, coach, and referee.

Once we became school age, my mother acted upon her strong desire to contribute to our often-depleted budget. She had a flair for coordinating colors, fabrics and designs and found pleasure in making clothes for her family. So she took a giant leap and applied for a job in the alterations department at a store downtown. This was the beginning of a thirty-year career in retail.

My father had six months remaining in his second term as Supervisor of Lauderdale County at his death. Married for forty-six years, at sixty-five years old my mother's focus shifted to completing his term. Her goal was to fulfill the remaining promises that he made to the constituents in his district.

During the last twelve years, Mama has consistently supported the youth in her community. She directed youth programs at New Hope Baptist Church, where she has been a member for fifty-two years. She has been involved in fundraising for the high school baseball team and she has worked tirelessly raising funds for the Martin Luther King, Jr. Scholarship Committee. Making sure the baseball team has the equipment necessary to ensure players' safety and presenting scholarships to deserving high school graduates has brought her immeasurable joy.

Mama continues to care deeply for her community. She supports efforts that will bring about peace and understanding. She also campaigns for candidates that she feels will best represent the interest of all people.

While Mama has deviated considerably from her upbringing of bare and unadorned, the threads of loving God, family and community are recognizable in her daily life. She has a passion for decorating her home and is overjoyed when friends and family are over for celebrations. She spends a few hours each day making necklaces to share with just about everyone she knows. Her personal indulgence is fashion. Mama has a special way of coordinating her accessories, shoes, handbags and clothes to create a look that is uniquely hers. My mother is radiant, she is sophisticated and she is so elaborate in everything that she does.

My brother, sister and I treasure the love and support that Mama lavishes upon us. All three of her grandchildren are touched in a special way by her manner of showing them her pride and joy in their lives. Her encouraging words, her lovely smile and the kindness in her voice continue to chase away any sadness and disappointments that we experience. I attempt to live my life in such a way to have the same impact on my children. I am so inspired when I hear her say, "I am blessed and the Lord has been faithful." ©

Kaye Sykes Williams and her husband, Jack, live in the East Bay, near San Francisco, where Kaye is an account manager for a State Farm Agent. They have two college-age children.

Kaye Sykes Williams and her mother, Laura Dean Lucas Sykes, at her mother's home, Meridian, Mississippi, 2014

It is good to have an end to journey towards; but it is the journey that matters, in the end. [38]

— URSULA K. LE GUIN,
The Left Hand of Darkness

Helena Rehfeldt

INVESTING IN THE FUTURE

At 80 years old, the author develops a new skill

My husband died unexpectedly when he was eighty-eighty and I was eighty, and I took over the management of our portfolio. The first time I called our broker and put in an order to sell, he chuckled and asked if I was planning on remodeling the kitchen or the master bath. Puzzled by his question, I didn't know what to say. He explained that so often he has noticed that new widows want to raise money for projects their husbands kept putting off. I laughed and told him I was doing a little financial housecleaning because I wanted to trade options. Silence.

That was nineteen years ago, and I can't say I have won on every deal, but I have done all right. My biggest disappointment came when *The Wall Street Journal* decided to stop printing the daily stock quotations. I wrote to the editorial staff on behalf of "The Greatest Generation," as Tom Brokaw calls us, because, in general, our eyesight is not as sharp as it was, and I thought we deserved a little consideration. I never received an answer. So I took out a subscription to *Investor's Business Daily*. While the paper quality isn't as good as that of *The WSJ,* and the print is not as crisp, with a magnifying glass, I have managed to make do. People have suggested I use the computer or fancy investment services, and I considered their advice carefully. I took a computer course and read about the services, but I have decided that I can keep ahead of the curve just as well sitting at the kitchen table with my pencil and my ruler.

In my ninety-nine years I have learned that change is part of life, but attitudes can be slow to give way. My brokers, both of them, have been supportive and encouraging. (They no longer ask me if I have a pencil to write something down or feel that they must caution me that a bond's maturity date is five years out.) But despite Gloria Steinem and Women's Lib, stereotyping survives. Recently my caregiver picked up the phone for me. She is faster on her feet than I am, and covering the receiver, she told me, "It's a man. It must be your doctor."

My doctor is a woman. It was my broker.

Helena Rehfeldt grew up on a dairy farm in Wisconsin and went east in 1941 to take a job caring for the daughter of a wealthy family in Manhasset. Her family said that if she changed her mind, they would happily pay her way back home. She fell in love with Manhattan, New York, became a New Yorker, and stayed fifty-seven years. In 2008, instead of moving south like most of her friends, she moved to Connecticut to be closer to her two daughters and two granddaughters. Helena lives with one of her daughters now and continues to invest, but she has never been published.*

*Editor's Note: Sadly, Helena Rehfeldt never saw her published narrative; she passed away, 100 years old, on August 4, 2015.

Helena Rehfeldt at home, 2013

ONE MORE TALE

Opening up to the pain of death, our own or that of someone we love, is one of the most mysterious blessings of life. Nothing focuses us more clearly on what matters, helps us drop our defenses more quickly or gives us more compassion for human suffering.[39]

— MARIANNE WILLIAMSON,
Illuminata

Marjorie Penn Lasky

THE INEVITABLE INTRUDES

The "Trip of Unintended Consequences" brings love –
and death – at 75

I was 73, almost 74, when I phoned him. After returning from my gru-eling hiking excursion in Sedona, I thought I was ready for another challenge – one more emotionally loaded than the compiling of the stories that appear here. Why not consider a relationship? I had divorced in the 1970s and spent decades "unpartnered" He was an old friend, someone with whom I had shared a crush and even a brief romance many years ago. We lived in the San Francisco area, usually on different sides of the Bay, and had stayed in touch over the years. He had married successfully for the second time and, in the late 1990s, had photographed my daughter's wedding. Every few years we conversed briefly, but we hadn't spoken in seven or eight years. His wife had developed Alzheimer's and, reluctantly, he had placed her in an institution the previous year. Emboldened yet apprehensive, I decided to call.

Surprised to hear from me, he thought a get-together was a great idea. On our second or third excursion, he declared there could be no romance as he very much loved his wife. No romance was actually okay with me because I realized I couldn't cope with the anxiety of an intimate relationship. I liked being with him. We had similar interests and he opened a whole new world to me, photography – not taking photos but learning to understand the works of people I had never heard of and new ways of seeing, e.g., footfalls, linear shadows, diagonal planes. We saw each other every two or three weeks. We exchanged emails (he didn't text), he sent photocopies of his photos through the U.S. mail and, sporadically and briefly, we talked on the phone. "Hanging out" together was intense with hours of ardent conversations. I never quite knew how to place my shoulders or arms next to him at a concert or a movie, but we managed. We dodged a couple romantic possibilities. I never told my friends or kids about him; after all, he was just another male friend and I feared anyone's pressuring me to consider whether it was more than that.

Eleven months after our first outing, a crisis occurred – his wife passed away. He was grief-stricken. And another crisis was brewing – one he knew about but didn't share, with anyone.

The day before I left for an extended trip to Japan, we spent two hours together.

During my trip, we emailed each other except for a week when he didn't write. He later wrote about being distracted.

My thoughts while traveling: He would probably go through a prolonged mourning period (perhaps a year or more) and eventually we might discover if we wanted something beyond a friendship. If we were lucky at our age (he, too, was almost 74), perhaps we'd have ten good years together.

But then, when is life ever so straightforward?

We made plans to see each other shortly after I returned home. He said he couldn't drive because he had a glitch with his eye. I assumed it was connected to his previous cataract surgery. Although he later told me he had practiced breaking the news to me for days, he simply blurted it out. The week he hadn't written, he had coils inserted in cranial veins because of fistulas. During his recovery, doctors discovered that the prostate cancer he had survived in 1999 had metastasized in the small bones behind one eye. He was finishing radiation to shrink the tumor; spots on his hip had been radiated. I reeled, quite literally. I couldn't stand up. I didn't know what fistulas were but I knew what bone metastasis from prostate cancer meant. My father had contracted and died from the disease and I had zealously researched it. Although Doug knew the situation was serious, he didn't comprehend the most likely outcome, and I was not about to tell him.

Two months later, his urologist told him that the Lupron shot, which he had received to slow the metastasis, didn't work. The doctor placed him in hospice. His wonderful daughter, who was with him when he heard the news, had to leave; he called and asked me to visit. I packed a change of clothes, a nightgown, and a toothbrush. I didn't leave him – almost literally – for nine months. The basic facts: He went into and then out of hospice, endured palliative chemo, attempted to enjoy a chemo holiday, underwent more radiation, reregistered with hospice, and passed away at home.

Why did I stay in a situation which was bound to bring me great sadness? After all, I had a choice. Before my return from Japan, none of my friends or family knew we had been "keeping company." Only a couple of his friends and his daughter knew about me. We weren't lovers. It would be and was a struggle, medically and emotionally. My home was 40 minutes by car from his – if I avoided rush hour – and I had to rent out part of my house to ensure that someone was there and yet remain able to return if I needed to do so. My garden required weekly attention. Friends cautioned me about becoming resentful given the level of care he would need. I never felt accepted by many of his friends, who could neither understand how I had come into his life nor envision him as a man separate from his late wife. And he never stopped loving her although he scrupulously tried to make me comfortable.

Yet, I couldn't leave him. I cared about him. He cared for me (he confided he had been most concerned about telling the news to two people – his daughter and me). His daughter couldn't take him in. I liked sleeping next to him. For some reason, I felt safe and my insomnia stopped. We had some amazingly poignant and joyful times together. We could make each other laugh (almost to the very end). I liked not having to reach out for company. Our honesty and his flexibility resolved potentially resentful situations, e.g., he would clean up the kitchen, allow my dog to sleep in the house, and take a taxi home after a minimally invasive medical visit. We learned, or tried, to live day-to-day and in the moment. We grew to love each other in a way that only "doomed" lovers can, engaging and disengaging simultaneously. His daughter and her family folded me into their lives. I grieve, not just for him but also for what the relationship might have become if circumstances had differed.

If I had previously known everything that would occur in living with and caring for Doug, I would have made the same decision. Although I didn't get what I had thought I wanted, by moving toward, not hiding from, the difficulties, I was stretched (dare I say challenged?) in unexpected ways – discovering unfamiliar skills, my heart expanded as I dealt with loving Doug and letting go.

Marjorie Lasky, Tiruvannamalai, India, 2012

Marjorie Lasky is Professor Emerita of history from the Contra Costa Community College District (California), where she was also a union activist and faculty union president. Although preferring to live in the moment, she has plans – to play her saxophone, to spend more time with friends and family, and to travel.

NOTES

[1] Naomi Shihab Nye, "The Man Who Makes Brooms," *Words under the words* (Portland, Oregon: Eighth Mountain Press, 1995), 127.

[2] Faye Wattleton quoted in Makers, "12 Quotes from Women That Will Inspire Activism," https://www.makers.com/blog/12-quotes-women-will-inspire-activism

[3] Ann Angel, *A Reader's Guide to Sandra Cisneros' The House on Mango Street* (Berkeley Heights, NJ: Enslow Publishers, Inc., 2010), 82. Original source footnoted in Angel (116) is Gayle Elliott, "An Interview with Sandra Cisneros," *Missouri Review*, Vol 25, November 1, 2002.

[4] Zora Neale Hurston, *Dust Tracks on a Road* (Thorndike, Maine: G. K. Hall & Co., 1997), 33. Large Print.

[5] Brandon French, "Forsaken," unpublished short story, email to editor, March 19, 2018.

[6] Anita Diamant, *The Red Tent* (New York: Picador, 1998), 2.

[7] Virginia Woolf, *A Room of One's Own*, (New York: Harcourt Inc., 1989), 76.

[8] Sherrilyn Kenyon, *Winter's Night* (New York: St. Martin's, 2015), Kindle Edition.

[9] Twyla Tharp, quoted in Robert Greskovic, "A Dance Master Does Dylan," *The Wall Street Journal,* September 25, 2017, https://www.wsj.com/articles/a-dance-master-does-dylan-1506370150

[10] Gloria E. Anzaldúa, *Borderlands/La Frontera: The New Mestiza* (San Francisco: Spinsters/Aunt Lute Book Company, 1987), 70.

[11] Faith Ringgold, quoted in Alexxa Gotthardt, "The Enduring Power of Faith Ringgold's Art," August 4, 2016, https://www.artsy.net/article/artsy-editorial-why-faith-ringgold-matters

[12] Julia Cameron, quoted in Sara Douchette, "25 quotes on Innovation and Creativity," 10 February 2015, https://www.wazoku.com/25-quotes-on-innovation-and-creativity/

[13] Willa Cather, *The Song of the Lark* (New York: Vintage Books, 1999), Part IV, Chapter 3, 279.

[14] Barbara De Angelis, *How Did I Get Here?: Finding Your Way to Renewed Hope and Happiness When Life and Love Take Unexpected Turns* (New York: St. Martin's Press, 2005), quoted in https://www.goodreads.com/author/quotes/72891.Barbara_De_Angelis

[15] Maya Angelou, *Letter to My Daughter* (New York: Random House, 2008), xii.

[16] Ruth Asawa, interview 1994, quoted in http://www.nytimes.com/2013/08/18/arts/design/ruth-asawa-an-artist-who-wove-wire-dies-at-87.html

[17] Phyllis Whitney, *Guide to Fiction Writing* (Boston: The Writer, Inc. Publishers, 1982), 5-6.

[18] Freya Stark, *The Journey's Echo: Selections from Freya Stark* (New York: Harcourt, Brace & World, 1964), 54.

[19] Rachel Naomi Remen, *My Grandfather's Blessings: Stories of Strength, Refuge, and Belonging* quoted in http://www.quotelady.com/subjects/risk.html

[20] Brené Brown, *The Gifts of Imperfection: Let Go of Who You Think You're Supposed to Be and Embrace Who You Are* (City Center, MN: Hazelden, 2010), 6.

[21] Anna Quindlen "Anna Quindlen quotes," quoted in https://www. goodreads.com/author/quotes/3500.Anna_Quindlen

[22] Marcia Schnedler, *The Seasoned Traveler* (Castine, Maine: Country Roads Press, 1992), ix.

[23] Ella Maillart, "Ella Maillart Quotes," http://www.azquotes.com/ author/9303-Ella_Maillart

[24] Agnes Repplier, *Times and Tendencies* (Boston: Houghton Mifflin, 1931), 142.

[25] Janet Kalven, "Respectable Outlaw," quoted in lebrun, k. (2008). Respectable Outlaw. Retrieved from http://www.trunity.net/ KWLsPortal/view/article/131139

[26] Ellen Johnson Sirleaf, "If Your Dreams Do Not Scare You, They Are Not Big Enough," Commencement Address, Harvard University, 2011, quoted in https://harvardmagazine.com/2011/05/ ellen-johnson-sirleaf-commencement-speech

[27] Anaïs Nin, *The Diary of Anaïs Nin, Volume 4: 1944-1947* (New York: Harcourt, 1971), 74.

[28] Dr. Mae Jemison, Twitter quote from White House Conference on STEM Education, https://twitter.com/maejemison/ status/792012595725303808

[29] Nadine Gordimer, quoted in Presentation Speech by Professor Sture Allén, "Award Ceremony Speech," https://www.nobelprize.org/ nobel_prizes/literature/laureates/1991/presentation-speech.html

[30] Delores Huerta, "Election Day is the Most Important Day of Your Life," quoted in ed. Joe Baker, *HuffPost*, October 27, 2016, https://www.huffingtonpost.com/entry/election-day-is-the-most-im- portant-day-of-your-life_us_5810eb7de4b06e45c5c70185

[31] Aretha Franklin, quoted in Michael Eric Dyson, "The Church of Aretha Franklin," *New York Times,* August 16, 2018, https://www.nytimes.com/2018/08/16/opinion/aretha-franklin-church-detroit.html

[32] Virginia Whitehill, *She's Beautiful When She's Angry*, Directed by Mary Dore, Chicago: Music Box Films, 2014. Film.

[33] Malala Yousafzai, "Malala Yousafzai speech in full" (New York, NY, United Nations, July 12, 2013), quoted in BBC News, http://www.bbc.com/news/av/world-asia-23291897/malala-yousafzai-speech-in-full.

[34] Germaine Greer, *The Change: Women, Aging and the Menopause* (New York: Alfred A. Knopf, 1992), 34.

[35] Elizabeth Janeway, "Breaking the Age Barrier," *Ms* (April 1973), quoted in "Barnard Alumnae," https://archive.org/stream/barnardalumnae624barn/barnardalumnae624barn_djvu.txt

[36] Anita Septimus, "The Ultimate List of Inspirational Travel Quotes," https://everything-everywhere.com the-ultimate-list-of-inspirational-travel-quotes/

[37] Nancy Thayer, *Morning* (Great Britain: Sphere Books Ltd., 1989), 249.

[38] Ursula K. Le Guin, *The Left Hand of Darkness* (New York: Ace Books, 1969), 220.

[39] Marianne Williamson, *Illuminata: Thoughts, Prayers, Rites of Passage,* (New York: Random House Ebook, 2013), 116.

INDEX OF CONTRIBUTORS